RAFFAELE MATTIOLI LECTURES

In honour of the memory of Raffaele Mattioli, who was for many years its manager and chairman, Banca Commerciale Italiana has established the Mattioli Fund as a testimony to the continuing survival and influence of his deep interest in economics, the humanities and sciences.

As its first enterprise the Fund has established a series of annual lectures on the history of economic thought, to be called the Raffaele Mattioli Lectures.

In view of the long association between the Università Commerciale Luigi Bocconi and Raffaele Mattioli, who was an active scholar, adviser and member of the governing body of the University, it was decided that the lectures in honour of his memory should be delivered at the University, which together with Banca Commerciale Italiana has undertaken the task of organising them.

Distinguished academics of all nationalities, researchers and others concerned with economic problems will be invited to take part in this enterprise, in the hope of linking pure historical research with a debate on economic theory and practical policy.

In creating a memorial to the cultural legacy left by Raffaele Mattioli, it is hoped above all that these lectures and the debates to which they give rise will prove a fruitful inspiration and starting point for the development of a tradition of research and academic studies like that already long established in other countries, and that this tradition will flourish thanks to the lasting partnership between the Università Commerciale Luigi Bocconi and Banca Commerciale Italiana.

AN EMPIRICALLY
BASED MICROECONOMICS

RAFFAELE MATTIOLI FOUNDATION

Herbert A. Simon

AN EMPIRICALLY BASED MICROECONOMICS

CAMBRIDGE
UNIVERSITY PRESS

CAMBRIDGE UNIVERSITY PRESS
Cambridge, New York, Melbourne, Madrid, Cape Town, Singapore, São Paulo, Delhi

Cambridge University Press
The Edinburgh Building, Cambridge CB2 8RU, UK

Published in the United States of America by Cambridge University Press, New York

www.cambridge.org
Information on this title: www.cambridge.org/9780521118361

First published 1997
This digitally printed version 2009

A catalogue record for this publication is available from the British Library

ISBN 978-0-521-62412-1 hardback
ISBN 978-0-521-11836-1 paperback

CONTENTS

PREFACE   XI

FIRST LECTURE

Rationality in Decision Making   3

   1. Development of the Concept of Rationality, pp. 3-13.
2. Contemporary Choice Theory, pp. 13-17.   3. The Plurality
of Rationalities, pp. 17-19.   4. The History Reviewed,
pp. 19-22.   5. Empirical Tests of Theories, pp. 22-23.

REFERENCES   23

DEBATE OF THE FIRST LECTURE   25

SECOND LECTURE

The Role of Organizations in an Economy   33

   1. Organizations and Markets, pp. 33-38.   2. Altruism and
Organizational Identification, pp. 38-45.   3. Organization,
Management, and the Economy, pp. 45-51.   4. Conclusion,
pp. 51-52.

REFERENCES   53

DEBATE OF THE SECOND LECTURE   54

THIRD LECTURE

Empirical Evidence for Economics   61

   1. How Much Theory, and How Concrete?, pp. 61-63.
2. Implications of Data for Theory, pp. 63-70.   3. The Sources
of Data on Economic Processes, pp. 70-71.   4. Seeking
Empirical Data Outside the Business Firm, pp. 71-81.
5. Decision Making in the Business Firm: Case Studies,
pp. 81-84.   6. Economic History, pp. 84-85.   7. Data from
"Applied" Economics, pp. 85-88.   8. Survey Techniques,
pp. 88-89.   9. Conclusion, pp. 89-91.

CONTENTS

REFERENCES 91

DEBATE OF THE THIRD LECTURE 94

COMMENTS 101

Claudio Dematté 103
Massimo Egidi 111
Robert Marris 133
Aldo Montesano 145
Riccardo Viale 153

SIMON'S REPLY 167

HERBERT A. SIMON'S AUTOBIOGRAPHYCAL SKETCH 189

BIBLIOGRAPHY 197

INDEX 217

PREFACE

I am grateful to the Università Commerciale Luigi Bocconi and the Banca Commerciale Italiana for inviting me to present my views on microeconomics, and especially on the kinds of empirical research that are going to be needed to assure its steady advancement. I am especially pleased at the opportunity this has given me to exchange ideas with a number of distinguished Italian economists in the question periods that followed my talks and in the final round-table discussion. Our interchange has enabled me to reassess my ideas, to change some of them, and to acquire new ones. My hosts at the Bank and the University also conspired to make my visit not only intellectually stimolating, but most pleasant as well.

In visits to Italy in the past decade, to Milano, Padova, Pavia, Roma, Siena, and Torino I have found, among the economists I have met, a strong spirit of innovation, and vigorous efforts to move economics in a behavioral direction and to strengthen greatly its empirical foundations. There is widespread recognition that economics needs closer and more direct contact with the phenomena it seeks to explain: that it must develop its methods for observing economic decision processes closely, inside business firms as well as in markets; must make more extensive use of symbolic computer simulation of these decision processes; and must expand its use of thinking-aloud protocols and other techniques for modeling decision making at a detailed level. I feel that empirically based behavioral economics is in excellent hands in your country, and I hope that these lectures will give additional support to the trends I saw there.

I want to thank all of those who were responsible for the arrangements of my visit, who participated in the discussion, and who assisted in the preparation of my lectures and the discussions for publication. I would like to mention, in particular, Professor Piero Tedeschi who, as the editor of this volume, oversaw the collection and revision of all the manuscripts and carried them safely through the final stages of publication.

Herbert A. Simon
Pittsburgh, Pennsylvania
June 18, 1996

HERBERT A. SIMON

AN EMPIRICALLY
BASED MICROECONOMICS

The *Raffaele Mattioli Lectures* were delivered by
Herbert A. Simon at the Università Commerciale Luigi Bocconi,
in Milano, from 18th to 19th March 1993.

FIRST LECTURE
Rationality in Decision Making

1. Development of the Concept of Rationality. – 2. Contemporary Choice Theory. – 3. The Plurality of Rationalities. – 4. The History Reviewed. – 5. Empirical Tests of Theories.

The concepts of reason and rationality are central to economics, but it must not be supposed that these concepts have retained the same meanings throughout the history of the subject. The assertion that "human beings behave rationally" may have a quite different meaning and carry quite different implications in the pages of Adam Smith than in those written by Kenneth Arrow or by an exponent of the rational expectations point of view. In my own writing, I have found it necessary to distinguish some of these different meanings of rationality, and in order to do so I have qualified the term by various adjectives: in particular, "bounded rationality", "substantive rationality", and "procedural rationality".

1. Development of the Concept of Rationality

Perhaps the easiest way to show what is at stake in the almost unperceived changes in meaning that have taken place over the past two hundred years is to compare and contrast the way in which the concept of rationality was used by Adam Smith with some of the changed usages that have appeared in succeeding years. This historical approach seems especially appropriate in the context of the Raffaele Mattioli Lectures, which are dedicated to treating economic topics in an historical context.

a. Introductory Comments on Writing History

Nowadays, in writing history we are sensitive to the danger of coloring our picture of the past with hindsight from the present. In English, we call that kind of distorted history "whiggish";

3

I don't know how to translate this term into Italian, and my dictionary does not help, for it equates "Whig" with "liberale" – quite another meaning.

A whiggish historian treats history as a tale of progress from an imperfect Past to a Present which, if not perfect, has at least moved perceptibly in the direction of perfection.

Moreover, in giving an account of the past, the whiggish historian will focus on those past developments that anticipated the present and led to it. In writing about the history of a science, it is particularly difficult to avoid whiggishness.

Most of us believe that the history of science *is* a story of progress: that for the most part the scientific knowledge of one century comes closer to an accurate and true description of the world than the knowledge of the previous century did. The continuing accumulation of empirical knowledge enables us to detect and correct errors in our beliefs, and the gradual development and revision of powerful explanatory theories pictures our world in increasingly accurate and parsimonious forms. And because we believe there is a progressive path in science, we dwell longer on those historical figures who marched along this path than on those who temporarily lured the march away from it. We focus on Galileo rather than on those of his contemporaries for whom the Earth stood still.

This view of inevitable progress has been challenged in our time by many historians, philosophers, and especially sociologists of science. The philosopher Feyerabend (1975) denies that our attempts to observe the world bring us continually nearer to a true view of it. There is no correct scientific method, he says, "Anything goes". Sociologists of science preach a cultural relativism. Changes in science, according to the relativists, are not a product of the internal processes of the disciplines: the accumulation of new knowledge, the generation and testing of alternative theories. Science, they argue, is simply a reflection of the society in which it exists: there is feudal science and Marxist science and capitalist science, male-dominated science and female-dominated science, and science of every racial and ethnic variety. Each is valid only within its social setting.

The historians of science, while opposing whiggishness, have generally been more moderate. They insist mainly that the science of a past century be examined in terms of the knowledge that the scientists of that time had inherited and had available to them, rather than in terms of the superior knowledge of later centuries. Without denying that the heliocentric view of the solar system has advantages over the geocentric view, they would explain why the latter might have seemed quite reasonable up to the time of Copernicus and Galileo, and why the shift of belief from theories we now regard as quite inadequate to more satis-factory theories sometimes takes considerable time. So, well-balanced accounts have now been given of the gradual resolution of the dispute between phlogisten-based and oxygen-based the-ories of combustion, and of the generation-long skepticism about Wegener's hypothesis of continental drift.

In my own account of the changed meanings of rationality within economics, I will try to follow this moderate course marked out by the historians of science. Without denying the possibility (perhaps even the fact) of progress, I will not treat Adam Smith as simply a primitive forerunner of contemporary theorists who are far superior: who not only have added many facts to those he had available, but also have clarified concepts that he could formulate only dimly. On the contrary, with re-spect to the notion of rationality, I will argue that Smith main-tained a clarity and consistency that has sometimes eluded his successors.

b. Rationality in The Wealth of Nations

As his title, *The Wealth of Nations*, clearly signals, Adam Smith's subject is not the internal world of the mind, but the external world of economic production and trade. He early (pp. 13-14; all references are to the 5th, 1789, edition) argues a close connection between productivity and the division of labor, and treats the lat-ter as "the necessary . . . consequence of a certain propensity in human nature . . .: the propensity to truck, barter, and exchange one thing for another". This latter he traces, in turn, to the mu-tual interdependence of people in civilized society. "But man has almost constant occasion for the help of his brethern, and it is in vain for him to expect it from their benevolence only. He will be more likely to prevail if he can interest their self-love in his favour, and shew them that it is for their own advantage to do for him what he requires of them ... It is not from the benevolence of the butcher, the brewer, or the baker, that we expect our dinner, but from their regard to their own interest".

Thus, the fundamental psychological assumptions of *The Wealth of Nations* are that, because of their dependence, human beings see the advantage to be gained from the help of others; and, because of their selfishness, they enter into mutually beneficial bargains. The term "rationality" does not enter explicitly into this discussion, and the *concept* enters only to the extent that effective selfishness depends upon being able to judge where self-interest lies.

Smith's world is a world of individual farmers, artisans, tradesmen, landowners. There is almost no place in it for the modern large manufacturing or service establishment. His division of labor is a specialization among participants in a market, not specialization of employees and managers in a business firm. He takes an extremely dim view of joint stock companies, except possibly in banking, insurance, or the provision of canals and water supplies (pp. 715-716). (His view of the inefficiency of universities, among the large corporations of his time, is especially scathing!) Therefore, *The Wealth of Nations* has little to say about the topic that will be central to my second and third lectures: the role of organizations in an economy.

Within his framework, Smith has no occasion to treat human choice or decision making in any formal way. (The term "self-interest" appears in his index, but not the terms "reason", "rationality", "choice", or "decision".) This does not mean that he regards people as non-rational; in fact, he frequently offers reasons for their behaving in particular ways. But in his treatment, being rational means having reasons for what you do. It does not imply maximizing anything, or having a single consistent criterion of choice, a utility, that provides the criterion for all decisions. A few examples will illustrate how Smith interprets human rationality.

In speaking of differences in wages between different skills, he says (p. 47): "Or if the one species of labour requires an uncommon degree of dexterity and ingenuity, the esteem which men have for such talents, will naturally give a value to their produce, superior to what would be due to the time employed about it. Such talents can seldom be acquired but in consequence of long application, and the superior value of their produce may frequently be no more than a reasonable compensation for the time and labour which must be spent in acquiring them".

The same theme is elaborated in the opening pages of chapter 8, where it is observed that wages vary with the agreeableness of the employment, the cost of learning the business, the constancy of employment, the trust to be reposed, and the probability of success. In each case, Smith states concisely the reasons for these differences and supplies numerous concrete examples. The theme of his remarks is that if people see a clear advantage in a particular course of action, they will seize it.

Similar common sense is applied to reasoning about the uses of capital: "...wherever a great deal can be made by the use of money, a great deal will commonly be given for the use of it ... The progress of interest, therefore, may lead us to form some notion of the progress of profit" (p. 88).

In all of these examples, the economic actors are certainly behaving rationally – that is, pursuing what they suppose to be their self-interest. They are doing this simply by observing the world around them and noting when one course of action is distinctly more advantageous than another. The quotations I have read show how cautiously Smith states his case, and how he qualifies his assertions with adverbs that indicate he claims only a general tendency. The pay for extra skill "*may frequently* be no more than a reasonable compensation for the time and labour", or "will *commonly* be given for the use of it". The rationality of *The Wealth of Nations* is the rationality of everyday common sense. It follows from the idea that people have reasons for what they do. It does not depend on an elaborate calculus of utility or assume any consistency in what factors are taken into consideration in moving from one choice situation to another.

One final comment on Smith's idea of self-interest: from his examples, we gather that self-interest frequently corresponds to economic gain. But he recognizes that people may respond to many other values: the attractiveness of an occupation may depend on the ease or pleasantness of its duties, the esteem or dishonor associated with it, and its risk to life and health. Moreover, Smith makes a great distinction between the prudent man and the prodigal, having very harsh words for the latter, not on grounds of individual values but because the prodigal does not contribute, by saving, to the nation's wealth and well-being.

Having contrasted (pp. 324-325) "the passion for present enjoyment" with the desire for an "augmentation of fortune" to better one's condition, he makes an empirical assertion that "though the principle of expence [i. e., expenditure for present enjoyment], therefore, prevails in almost all men upon some occasions, and in some men upon almost all occasions, yet in the greater part of men, taking the whole course of their life at an average, the principle of frugality seems not only to predominate, but to predominate very greatly . . . Great nations are never impoverished by private, though they sometimes are by public prodigality". He then adduces historical examples to buttress this claim further.

This burst of optimism is the closest that Smith comes to defining a utility function, one balancing the propensity to consume against the propensity to save. *The Wealth of Nations* has a clear normative mission. It is not only a theoretical and empirical inquiry into "the nature and causes of the wealth of nations", but also a strong advocate for the policies that will increase that wealth. It contains no similar advocacy of individual rationality – a satisfactory level of rationality is taken for granted. Its only expressed preference for individual conduct, as contrasted with public policy, is for a particular shape of the utility function – a shape that will subordinate current consumption to saving!

Everything that psychology has learned about the processes of human choice is consistent with the view expressed by Adam Smith. People do have reasons for what they do, but these reasons depend very much on how people frame or represent the situations in which they find themselves, and upon the information they have or obtain about the variables that they take into account. Their rationality is a procedural rationality; there is no claim that they grasp the environment accurately or comprehensively. To predict their behavior in specific instances, we must ourselves know what they are attending to, and what information they have.

c. Rationality in Marshall's Principles

We jump ahead now a little more than a century, and take Alfred Marshall's *Principles of Economics* (8th edition, 1920) as a summing up of of that century's remarkable output of economic discussion and theory. Marshall himself, in the Preface to the first edition of his book, emphasizes the continuity of economics from its beginnings and selects as the most salient advance from earlier times the introduction of marginal concepts, which he attributes especially to Cournot, von Thuenen and Jevons.

The opening pages of *Principles*, however, show other important shifts in emphasis: in particular, a shift from national wealth to the activities of mankind "in the ordinary business of life". Several of his introductory sentences are worth quoting (pp. 1-3).

"Thus [economics] is on the one side a study of wealth; and on the other, and more important side, a part of the study of man. For man's character has been moulded by his every-day work, and the material resources which he thereby procures, more than by any other influence unless it be that of his religious ideals. ... And very often the influence exerted on a person's character by the amount of his income is hardly less ... than that exerted by the way in which it is earned".

The theme of an intimate interaction between economic institutions and activities, on the one hand, and individual character, on the other, is developed still further in a discussion of the conditions of modern industrial life (pp. 5-6). "[These characteristics are] ... a certain independence and habit of choosing one's own course for oneself, a self-reliance; a deliberation and yet a promptness of choice and judgment, and a habit of forecasting the future and of shaping one's course with reference to distant aims ... [The resultant tendencies toward collective ownership and collective action] are the result ... of free choice by each individual of that line of conduct which after careful deliberation seems to him the best suited for attaining his ends, whether they are selfish or unselfish". To emphasize further the lack of connection between rationality and selfishness, Marshall observes (p. 6) that, "that country [England] which is the birthplace of modern competition devotes a larger part of its income than any other to charitable uses, and spent twenty millions on purchasing the freedom of the slaves in the West Indies".

Central to these passages of Marshall is the phrase: ". . . free choice by each individual of that line of conduct which after careful deliberation seems to him the best suited for attaining his ends, whether they are selfish or unselfish". This statement incorporates two major departures of Marshall's analysis from that of Adam Smith. First, the rather informal approach to choice by human beings "who have reasons for what they do", is replaced by emphasis upon deliberation in decision making, which in *Principles* becomes marginal analysis and maximization of utility. Second, and consistently with the idea that utility can be filled with any wishes or wants whatsoever, so long as they are consistent, Marshall does not insist on self-interest as the main driver of action. Utility can derive from altruistic as well as selfish choices; economics does not postulate or predict what things will have utility or how much they will have.

While Marshall puts forth nothing resembling Adam Smith's unbuttressed assertion that frugality will dominate profligacy, yet in a long passage he purports to give a (very generalized) historical account of "the slow and fitful development of the habit of providing for the future" (pp. 220-229), which reaches a conclusion as optimistic as Smith's about the prospects for the cumulation of capital in a modern society. The habit of reckoning about the future becomes another component of Marshallian rationality. Marshall's people form expectations, the progenitors of today's "rational expectations".

The pages of Smith and Marshall covering the same topics reveal a vast difference between them even when their conclusions are almost identical (as they usually are). Although *The Wealth of Nations* is addressed to the "nature and causes" of wealth, one feels a dominant concern with policy issues, specifically, a concern with how to assure rapid growth in the national wealth. In *Principles*, one feels a dominant preoccupation with abstract technical analysis of the working of the economic system.

It is not that Marshall was unconcerned about normative matters; many of his other writings demonstrate his deep interest in them. But except for some *obiter dicta* along the way, about the efficiency of competitive markets and the beneficent effects of the accumulation of capital, he is largely preoccupied with showing how the method of partial equilibrium, with its careful *ceteris paribus* assumptions, can be used to predict the effects of shifts in supply or demand curves in response to policy decisions or other exogenous forces. Although he tries to deal with some welfare questions with the aid of the doctrine of consumer and producer surplus, these concepts have not survived very well subsequent neoclassical skepticism about interpersonal comparability of utility.

Books III and V of *Principles* are the main heritage that Marshall bequeathed to contemporary economics, the former developing the theory of utility maximization, the latter the theory of markets and partial equilibrium analysis. These are the most abstract sections of the book, and the ones containing the fewest references to facts or data of any kind. They are the sections that have the most contemporary feel.

It has more than once been noticed that Marshall's emphasis on partial equilibrium leads, implicitly or explicitly, to full employment of resources, and is therefore more relevant to microeconomics than to macroeconomics. *Principles* contains minimal discussion of money, and almost none of what we would call monetary policy – that is, the relation of money to the level of economic activity. Similarly, there is almost no consideration of the trade cycle (it and equivalent terms do not appear in the index). We find only some statements roughly equivalent to Say's Law, and a suggestion that temporary stagnation at less than full employment equilibrium could be caused by "lack of confidence" among employers and investors (pp. 710-711).

Marshall himself was aware of these limitations, but relegated macroeconomic dynamics largely to other books. Whatever his intentions, the consequence of this treatment of the economy as a whole was to bring about a greater separation than had previously existed of macroeconomics from microeconomics. The widespread use of *Principles* as a textbook and its enormous influence on the profession contributed much to reinforcing this separation.

Book IV of *Principles* is strikingly different from the Books that precede and follow it, resembling *The Wealth of Nations* in setting forth a large number of anecdotal "facts" in support of its descriptions of economic institutions. In particular, in chapters 8 through 13 of Book IV, Marshall gives an account of the rise of modern industrial organization, explaining on economic grounds the strong tendency for production to concentrate in large factories.

Of course the joint-stock company, of which Adam Smith was so disdainful, plays a large role in this story. While Smith argued that the managers of such companies would selfishly betray the interests of the stockholders ("mislead and impose upon" are his words); Marshall, although acknowledging the powerlessness of the shareholders, comments optimistically that "[i]t is a strong proof of the marvellous growth in recent times of a spirit of honesty and uprightness in commercial matters, that the leading officers of great public companies [i. e., joint stock companies] yield as little as they do to the vast temptations to fraud which lie in their way . . . There is every reason to hope that the progress of trade morality will continue . . . and thus collective and democratic forms of business management may be able to extend themselves safely in many directions in which they have hitherto failed, and may far exceed the great services they already render in opening a large career to those who have no advantages of birth (pp. 303-304) ".

Again, we find Marshall abandoning an assumption of pure selfishness, and postulating that other values, in this case "a spirit of honesty", provide the necessary motives and "utilities". With loyalty to the business interests thus assured, Marshall is able to use his marginal reasoning to argue that there are "some good reasons for believing that in Modern England the supply of business ability in command of capital accommodates itself, as a general rule, to the demand for it; and thus has a fairly defined supply price" (p. 313). This passage, and similar ones, can be viewed as harbingers of the present-day "new institutional economics", which seeks to explain the modern business firm within a framework of neoclassical assumptions and analysis.

With Marshall we see a reliance on reasoning from the premises of utility maximization and maximum efficiency in a way that is quite rare in Adam Smith. We see *citations* of fact fading into a place of secondary importance, and the specific case studies and historical accounts of Smith largely being replaced by *stipulations* of fact of a much more general and vague nature.

2. Contemporary Choice Theory

Finally, we leap forward another century, to see what has become of the theory of decision making in our own age. In the article on Economics written by Albert Rees for the *International Encyclopedia of the Social Sciences* (1968), we find (4:472) the following definition: "Economics . . . is the study of the allocation of scarce resources among unlimited and competing uses".

Here, at least momentarily, human beings and both their wants and their decision processes have disappeared from view. We are faced with a technical allocation problem, and are tempted to turn immediately to our linear programming algorithm to solve the problem. In fairness I must add that the definition just quoted is followed immediately by the supplementary statement that "[economics] is the social science that deals with the ways in which men and societies seek to satisfy their material needs and desires, since the means at their disposal do not permit them to do so completely".

The trends that took us from Adam Smith to Alfred Marshall have persevered in the same direction through a second century. The abstraction of the utility function is now complete, and the task now is not merely to allocate resources, but to allocate them efficiently, that is, in such a way that the utility of no member of the society can be increased further without decreasing the utility of at least one other member.

The separation of microeconomics from macroeconomics

remains, as in Marshall, nearly complete. Following Frank Knight (1921), Rees lists the "functions of an economy" as: (a) determining the composition of output; (b) organizing production; (c) distributing the product (or income); (d) providing for the future; and (e) allocating a fixed stock of goods over short periods of time (4:474). "Later", he continues "we shall turn to the discussion of money, the price level, and the level of unemployment, which, as noted earlier, lie largely outside the resource allocation framework".

Until Keynes (1936), macroeconomics remained a peripheral topic in standard general economics textbooks, a somewhat embarrassing left-over, relegated mostly to specialists in monetary theory. The realities of the Great Depression and Keynes' *General Theory* brought macrotheory to the center of the stage; but it is no secret today that Keynes was able to bring about a semblance of unity between his theory of underemployment and the Marshallian framework only by means of specific assumptions that had no place within the theory itself, and seemed to violate the increasingly rigorous assumptions of rationality that the neoclassicists were insisting upon.

If one examines closely the structure of *The General Theory*, one finds in it three quite distinct kinds of argumentation. First, a large part of the book is an exercise in neoclassical analysis. The assumptions and the modes of reasoning from them would not be at all out of place in the pages of Marshall's *Principles*. As Keynes puts it (p. 178), "Our criticism of the accepted classical theory of economics has consisted not so much in finding logical flaws in its analysis as in pointing out that its tacit assumptions are seldom or never satisfied, with the result that it cannot solve the economic problems of the actual world". Without this acceptance of marginalist methods of thought, *The General Theory* would not have had the enormous and relatively quick impact that it had on the thinking of mainstream economists. Keynes was one of them, and was challenging them on their own territory, in their own language.

But there is the second element in *The General Theory*, alluded to in the quotation from Keynes above. He challenged the real-world validity of key assumptions of the neoclassical framework by asserting that people are not always wholly rational. The deviations from perfect rationality that he proposes are of several forms, among the most prominent being the money illusion of workers, the inability of businessmen to form correct ("rational"?) expectations about future prospects, and the minimum rate of interest for investment. It was lapses from rationality of these sorts that brought about departures from full employment of resources, and that could be remedied by appropriate governmental policies.

Keynes' "yes-but" strategy: embracing the main body of classical theory, but modifying some key assumptions of rationality, also afforded a target for counterattack by theorists seeking to defend the classical stronghold. *The General Theory* could be interpreted as an account of short-run departures from the ultimately inevitable full-employment equilibrium. It was not too many years after the publication of Keynes' work that a vigorous cottage industry grew up among neoclassical economists, aiming to show how underemployment could be accommodated in the framework of rational calculation as a temporary dynamic departure from full-employment equilibrium. If Keynes could not be ignored, he could be eaten and digested. The absorption was the more easily accomplished because Keynes himself had departed from neoclassicism only to the minimal extent necessary to provide some mechanisms for unemployment.

But there is a third strand in *The General Theory* that suggests a more radical departure from the classical framework. A treatment of the whole economy and of dynamics leads quite naturally to a concern with the way people form expectations about the future. The topic of expectations was not unknown to Smith or to Marshall, but chiefly in relation to discussions of capital formation and the balance between present and future satisfactions. The crucial destabilizing effects that expectations (a form of feed-forward) can have on a dynamic system were not within their focal vision.

In Chapter 12, we find Keynes' famous comment (I am tempted to say "outburst") on "animal spirits". He observes (pp. 161-162) that, "even apart from the instability due to speculation, there is the instability due to the characteristic of human nature that a large proportion of our positive activities depend on spontaneous optimism rather than on a mathematical expectation, whether moral or hedonistic or economic. Most, probably, of our decisions to do something positive, the full consequences of which will be drawn out over many days to come, can only be taken as a result of animal spirits – of a spontaneous urge to action rather than inaction, and not as the outcome of a weighted average of quantitative benefits multiplied by quantitative probabilities. Enterprise only pretends to itself to be mainly actuated by the statements in its own prospectus, however candid and sincere. Only a little more than an expedition to the South Pole, is it based on an exact calculation of benefits to come ".

Although this passage is directed primarily at the formation of expectations, it constitutes a general challenge to the claim that we can predict economic behavior by determining what the globally rational utility maximizer would do. Only the fear of pronouncing an egregious anachronism prevents me from claiming Keynes, the author of this ringing statement, as the true originator of the economics of bounded rationality.

Except for the work of monetary theorists, serious concern with the question of how expectations are actually formed was slow in coming to economics. Apart from pioneers like Frank Knight (1921)and Albert Hart (1940), the list of mainstream economists working on these problems before World War II is not large. Then came a great burgeoning of interest, perhaps not unrelated to the appearance on the scene of control theory, statistical decision theory and game theory, as well as the desire, fueled by the appearance of electronic computers, to build large models for forecasting economic activity.

It was not long before the postulates (I resist calling them "tentacles") of rationality stretched out to embrace uncertainty – first in the form of adaptive expectations and then in the assumption of so-called rational expectations. Views of the future were themselves to be formed in an "optimal" way. I do not propose to discuss these doctrines, or their plausibility as descriptions of real human behavior. I call attention to them only as evidence of the strength of the economic profession's drive to embrace all of economic analysis, macro as well as micro, within the neoclassical framework.

3. The Plurality of Rationalities

This sketchy, but I hope not inaccurate, historical account makes evident how great has been the change since 1776 in the economist's assumptions about the rationality of economic actors: both with respect to the nature of their wants and needs, the shape and content of the utility function, and with respect to the deliberateness, comprehensiveness and subtlety of their calculations. Let me use the taxonomy suggested earlier to bring some order into this scene.

First, I have referred to the distinction between global rationality and bounded rationality. These terms have become familiar in the debates of the past several decades, and don't require extensive discussion. Global rationality, the rationality of neoclassical theory, assumes that the decision maker has a comprehensive, consistent utility function, knows all the alternatives that are available for choice, can compute the expected value of utility associated with each alternative, and chooses the alternative that maximizes expected utility. Bounded rationality, a rationality that is consistent with our knowledge of actual human choice behavior, assumes that the decision maker must search for alternatives, has egregiously incomplete and inaccurate knowledge about the consequences of actions, and chooses actions that are expected to be satisfactory (attain targets while satisfying constraints). The assumption that rationality is bounded leads in many cases to quite different conclusions about the operation of the economy than does the assumption of global rationality.

But if anyone still needs persuasion that the concept of bounded rationality is required for economic analysis, especially in the context of uncertainty, I recommend the 1987 article of Kenneth Arrow, which is also reprinted in *The New Palgrave Dictionary of Economics*. Perhaps they will find the testimony of one of the masters of modern equilibrium analysis more persuasive than arguments from someone who has always been skeptical of the neoclassical synthesis.

Within the framework of global rationality, we assume a given set of alternatives and a given utility function and compute the alternative that maximizes utility (or, in the case of uncertainty, subjective expected utility). Within the framework of bounded rationality, we assume that people have some goals and constraints and search for an alternative that reaches the goals, subject to the constraints and within specified limits on the knowledge and computational capacities and skills of the decision maker. In particular, the search may include a search for new alternatives and even for a new representation (frame of reference, context) within which to formulate the choice problem.

With global rationality, the properties of the decision maker, other than his or her utility function, disappear from the problem, so that we need no psychological theory other than a theory of human wants and needs, and in particular we need no understanding of human thought processes, in order to carry out economic analysis. On the other hand, with bounded rationality, we need both a sociology and a psychology of the decision maker to predict behavior – a sociology to tell us what information is likely to be available in memory at the time of decision and what needs and wants are likely to be prominent, and a psychology to tell us how the decision will be represented and how elaborate are the calculations that the decision maker can and will carry out in order to make a choice.

This leads to the second distinction: that between substantive and procedural rationality. The former is concerned only with finding what action maximizes utility in the given situation, hence is concerned with analyzing the situation but not the decision maker. It is a theory of decision environments (and utility functions), but not of decision makers. Procedural rationality is concerned with *how* the decision maker generates alternatives of action and compares them. It necessarily rests on a theory of human cognition.

There is a connection between the pair global-substantive rationality, on the one hand, and bounded-procedural rationality, on the other, because flesh-and-blood human beings have very limited capacities for knowledge and computation. Global rationality is substantive – it responds to the actual, objective characteristics of the decision situation. But it is only feasible if the situation is sufficiently simple so that human decision makers can apprehend the objective solution. In more complicated situations (most situations of practical interest) human bounded rationality requires that we understand the decision procedures if we are to predict behavior. A theory of bounded rationality is necessarily a theory of procedural rationality.

It is, of course, a great pity that a theory of global, substantive rationality will not do the job. If it would, we would be spared a tiresome inquiry into the sociology and psychology of human decision making. If wishes were horses, beggars would ride. But in the complex world in which we live, we are beggars and horseless. In a wide range of important situations, we cannot understand economic behavior without a correct theory of the processes and knowledge the actors are actually using to make their choices.

4. The History Reviewed

Let us now review the three moments in economic theory that I have described, to see where they stand on the global-bounded and substantive-procedural dimensions.

Adam Smith makes no assumption of a globally rational utility maximizer. He does assume a predominately selfish decision maker, which assumption does a great deal to narrow down the alternatives available. Beyond that he makes commonsense assumptions, specific to the particular trading, hiring, investing and other economic situations he is discussing, about how economic actors will view these situations, and what knowledge they will bring to bear on them.

Where does he get this information about his actors? He generates a great deal of it by empathy: he is a member of the culture to which his actors belong; he can put himself in their places and judge, perhaps not too inaccurately, what information they might have, what part of it they might take into consideration, and how they would use it to reason to their conclusions. In addition, Adam Smith spent enormous time and effort over many years to gather all the information he could lay his hands on about economic affairs in Britain and abroad, in his own time and in historical times. He could test and qualify his own empathetic "computations" against this body of knowledge.

This method of providing an empirical basis for theory is as old as human experience. Nowadays, we are very suspicious of it, because it appears so much less accurate and specific than controlled experiments or systematic observations guided by careful sampling. It provides only modest defenses against subjectivity. All of these objections may be admitted, but we must judge the method against its alternatives. The only real alternative for Smith was to try to draw conclusions about the same situations without use of either his knowledge or his empathetic powers. That surely would have been a losing strategy.

We conclude that Adam Smith used, if implicitly, an assumption of bounded rationality, but that he lacked the means for testing in any systematic way the knowledge and procedures that he thought his actors used in reaching their decisions. He certainly did not draw his conclusions by applying a rigorous model of utility maximization – the very idea was unknown to him – nor did he use modern empirical methods. There are few precise data (and, of course, no regressions) in *The Wealth of Nations*.

In the case of Marshall, we see a major shift toward a formal theory of global rationality as the foundation for analysis. This was possible when he placed at the focus of his attention the formation of prices and the responses of buyers and sellers to them, and made strong *ceteris paribus* assumptions to limit the range of consequences considered by the actors.

These assumptions were, of course, also a considerable step in the direction of introducing bounds upon rationality, but Marshall provided no computational or procedural theory to formalize this simplification or to determine which variables could validly be held constant. Like Smith, when it was necessary to assume something about an actor's utility function, he used "common sense" – i. e., empathy and general knowledge – to make the required assumptions. Marshall's common sense constructed much less selfish actors than did Smith's. A strong note of optimism about human motives runs through the *Principles*.

Contemporary neoclassical theory goes even farther in the direction explored by Marshall. A set of assumptions is created to define or "model" a decision situation. The model is treated as a description of reality; actually it is a highly simplified skeleton of reality trimmed down to the boundaries of the knowledge and computational limits of the theorist. If they are required (and they usually are), additional assumptions are made about the utilities of the decision maker, usually in terms of desires for goods and money.

The model itself is manipulated with great mathematical formality, and if it is tested with quantitative data, high standards of sophistication are imposed on the statistical methods employed. What is omitted is any serious testing of the validity of the assumptions of the model itself, even the kind of historical, experiential and anecdotal testing that we find in Smith and Marshall. This might be all right if the quantitative, econometric tests were generally sharp and decisive. Almost always, they are not.

The literature of modern economics is full of examples of the sensitivity of models to small changes of assumptions – many, if not most of them beyond the limits of accuracy of statistical tests. The Coase Theorem is a case in point. Simply by introducing into the awarenesses of the actors property rights in externalities, we allow them to bargain for the production or suppression of these externalities and reach new equilibria that have different welfare and distributive implications from the previous equilibria.

Similar sensitivities appear in the theory of incidence of urban property taxes. Harry Gunnison Brown (1924), by observing that such taxes (if the actors happened to think about the situation in the "right" way) could be shifted in part to capital in general (and not simply to capital invested in the property taxed), undermined the whole received theory of incidence that had been developed by Edgeworth, Seligman and Pierson. Some thirty years later, Tiebout (1956) brought about a new revolution in the theory by observing that the incidence would be different if householders took into account their mobility in or out of the taxed area.

The new models, once discovered, obviously represented a "higher" level of rationality than the old – they took account of a wider range of variables of the real world, with less *ceteris paribus*. However, it would be a fallacy to interpret this as meaning that the more sophisticated models are empirically the more correct. On the contrary, in the course of history economic actors may change their ways of looking at choice situations, just as economists do, and their decisions may thereby change. A theory based on global rationality would assume that the more sophisticated theory represents reality. From the viewpoint of bounded, procedural rationality, empirical evidence about how the economic actors view the situation and what factors play a role in their decisions would determine which theory is the correct one.

An interesting sequence recurs frequently in the literature on unemployment. Shortly after any new theory is published on this topic, another article appears showing that the unemployment predicted by the new theory only arises because one of the economic actors is behaving with less than global rationality (recall Keynes's emphasis on the money illusion of workers, or Lucas's on the money illusion of businessmen in explaining the underemployment of resources). This observation that the theory incorporates bounded rationality is regarded as refuting the theory. Of course it does not refute it. What it does is simply to raise the empirical question of whether the limit of rationality postulated by the theory is present in the real world. This is a question to be decided by evidence, not by applying the assumption of global utility maximization.

5. Empirical Tests of Theories

Our discussion focuses attention on the empirical testing of our theories. Historically, we have had two kinds of tests. First, there are the "commonsense" and experience-based tests employed so widely by Adam Smith – and, in fact, by all economists up to the present day. Second, there are the tests provided by econome-trics, applicable when appropriate quantitative data are available. Neither of these kinds of empirical tests of theory have proved so powerful (to understate the matter grossly) that we can feel satisfied with them. Is there an alternative?

The alternative is to test the validity of some or all of the specific assumptions that are built into the models as well as the models as wholes. There are at least two ways in which this can be done. As demonstrated extensively by Vernon Smith, and more recently by others, many market situations can be tested empirically in the laboratory, where particular variables can be controlled. I don't mean that such testing is simple or without its problems, but it has now been clearly demonstrated to be a pow-erful source of new empirical information about the behavior of participants in markets.

A second source of data is from empirical studies that observe the behavior of consumers or of business firms directly. Although there is a long history of sampling studies of consumer prefer-ences, beliefs and opinions, and, on a smaller scale, of decision making in individual business firms, there has been little use of such data – especially the case studies – to test economic theories.

In my third lecture, I will return to this topic and examine in greater detail how we can advance our methods for testing the empirical correctness of economic theories at both microeco-nomic and macroeconomic levels.

REFERENCES

ARROW Kenneth J., Rationality of self and others in an economic sys-tem, in HOGARTH, R. M. and REDER M. W. (eds.), *Rational Choice: the Contrast Between Economics and Psychology*, Chicago: University of Chicago Press, 1987.

BROWN Harry Gunnison, *Economics of Taxation*, New York: Henry Holt, 1924.

FEYERABEND Paul K., *Against Method*, London: NLB, 1975.

HART Albert G., *Anticipations, Uncertainty and Dynamic Planning*, New York: Kelley, 1940.

KEYNES John Maynard, *The General Theory of Employment, Interest and Money*, London: MacMillan & Co., 1936.

KNIGHT Frank H., *Risk, Uncertainty and Profit*, London: London School of Economics and Political Science, 1921 [1933].

MARSHALL Alfred, *Principles of Economics*, 8th edition. New York: The Macmillan Company, 1920.

REES Albert, Economics, in *International Encyclopedia of the Social Sciences* 4:472-485. New York: The Macmillan Company, 1968.

RICARDO David, *On the Principles of Political Economy and Taxation*, 2nd edition, London: John Murray, 1819.

SMITH Adam, *The Wealth of Nations*, 5th edition. New York: The Modern Library, 1789 [1937].

TIEBOUT C. M., A pure theory of local expenditures, *Journal of Political Economy* 64; 416-424, 1956.

DEBATE OF THE FIRST LECTURE

Interventions by Andrea Ichino, Luigi Pasinetti and others.

QUESTION. Can you clarify the relationship between full rationality, bounded rationality and procedural rationality?

SIMON. Neoclassical theory, put in the simplest terms, proceeds as though the facts of the real world are known. For the economic theorist but also the decision maker, there is a real world out there; people who are acting in it know about that world. They are able to calculate the consequences of their actions in the real world (or at least to act as if they had calculated them – Friedman would insist on that qualification). This is what I call full or global rationality: people are making their decisions to maximize utility in a world which they either understand exactly or in terms of a known probability distribution (i.e., they are maximizing subjective expected utility).

Bounded rationality says that each one of us, faced with living and making decisions, looks out in the world and tries to get a picture of it; and each one of us of course gains a different picture. It is a very approximate picture, usually with many errors in it, but certainly an extremely simple picture compared with everything in the world. We make very imperfect forecasts, and these are not even calculated using probability distributions but focus on just a few variables. For example, 15 years ago in the US, when people made decisions about their daily lives and how they should use their income and so forth, they didn't concern themselves with the price level. Then with the oil shocks, people became conscious of prices. As a result, the whole structure of their decision making changed, because they took new variables into account when they were deciding upon buying a new home or saving money or spending money. It was not so much that the world changed, as that the part of the world that was in their conscious awareness changed, and that made differences in their decisions. That is the difference between global rationality and bounded rationality.

Now, if you think people can deal with the world as it really is, so that you do not have to worry about their subjective view of it, then in order to predict their behavior you simply calculate what would maximize utility in that real world: you simply carry out a maximization exercise, applying linear programming or the like. We will call that substantive rationality – what would really be rational in the real world. If you believe, however, that our minds are very limited, that we can only form a very approximate picture of our world, then in order to predict our behavior you need a theory of how we make our decisions: you need a theory of procedural rationality.

Does that lead to a theory of the mind? Yes, indeed it does. Unless we have a theory of how the human mind operates, we have few grounds on which to build an economic theory that will talk about the kind of uncertain world we live in: that will understand inflation, that will understand savings behavior, that will understand motivations in the work place. I believe that we have made great progress toward building a theory of human thinking in the last 30 years, and therefore I am optimistic about the opportunities to apply it to economics. Some of that will come out in my later talks.

QUESTION. I think that rationality should be a purely subjective concept, while bounded rationality is still an objective one. Can you comment on this point?

SIMON. Bounded rationality is subjective in the sense that it is rationality as viewed by the decision maker. It is objective only in the sense that we (the economists) are trying to determine how the decision maker in fact makes his or her choices. We know from watching our own behavior and the behavior of our friends that there are all kinds of departures from what we would call objective rationality. Sigmund Freud showed that even madmen have reasons for what they do, although the reasons may not appeal to us because the framework in which the reasoning is done seems very strange to us. I am not pleading here for a particular theory of rationality; I am pleading here for an economics that seeks out the facts of how people do react to situations and tries to base economic theories on those facts rather than on speculations made in an armchair. We are only going to get those facts by expanding our methods of empirical study to include the study of what people do inside the business firm – not to exclude other kinds of behavior but to include that kind of behavior. I do not want to prejudge the outcome of doing that, otherwise we would not need the study.

We cannot simply assume that human beings will do those things that are objectively rational, or even those things that economists think are objectively rational. We have to find out how, in fact, people do make their decisions; and if those decisions include elements, as they surely do, that we would not by any stretch of definition call rational, so be it. Then we have to find a way to incorporate those decisions also in economic theory. We have to find ways of accounting for people's foolish ways, just as we account for events that seem more ordinary to us.

QUESTION. I think you read Smith's work using Marshall's interpretation. Is my understanding of your lecture correct? If so, can you comment on that?

SIMON. I am pleased to have a comment from someone who is much more learned in economic history than I pretend to be. One of my concerns in preparing this particular lecture was that I have no reason to regard myself as an historian of economic doctrine; and if I have not committed any worse errors than the one you mentioned, I am lucky – I have gotten away nearly free!

I think your remark is well aimed. Perhaps at the expense of the whiggishness which I warned against, I did look back at Adam Smith in terms of our concerns today and through the narrow focus of Marshall and particularly of his Principles; and I do not make any pretense of giving a view of what Adam Smith was aiming at, and in particular the development of his interest in policy proposals. In limiting myself to a discussion of human rationality I certainly gave a very partial view of Adam Smith. As I pointed out, that term is not even mentioned in his index, and it certainly was not a focal concept in his view of the world. Yet Smith was talking about human beings trying to advance their own economic interests; he was talking about self interest as a major motor that made the economic system operate, and it was this particular point that I was focusing on.

I was admiring the fact that Adam Smith made use of the kinds of empirical knowledge that were available in his time, and very good use of them. There is a marvellous passage in *The Wealth of Nations* in which he looks at the comparative cost of hauling coal from the Midlands down to London by barge, versus by dray on the roads. I think operations researchers today would have been proud to have carried out that particular analysis. So he made very good use of the empirical knowledge that was available to him or that he could put together at his time.

I am not proposing that we go back to doing that, either for Adam Smith's purposes or for our own, because today we do have and can have other sources of data, other ways of establishing our empirical facts. But I did want, in this rather limited view I gave of Adam Smith – a view from the standpoint only of decision making – I did want to show that economics has not always been in its present state of trying to reach its conclusions from logical premises with little intervention of fact. Facts played a large role in Adam Smith's analysis.

QUESTION. I present you two stories. The first one: "A man is searching for his watch at night under the light of a lamppost, and people ask him, 'Why do you search here if you do not know whether you lost the watch here or somewhere else?' The man answers: 'Well I search here because here I have the light'".

The second story is: "A king wants a map of his kingdom, and asks the prime minister for a map. The prime minister comes back with a map, let us say with a scale 200.000:1, and the king is very upset; he cannot see his palaces, his towns, his castles and so on. Therefore, the King asks for a different map at a bigger scale . . . The story goes on until finally the Prime Minister comes back with a map 1:1". That is totally useless. Can the debate on full rationality (neoclassical economics) and bounded rationality be represented metaphorically by these two stories?

SIMON. I think you have given a very clear statement of the debate that is increasingly going on between those who defend neoclassical economics and some of us who have less patience with it. I think those are exactly the kinds of issues in terms of which the debate has been framed.

Let me talk about the stories first, and then I will have a word to say on teaching the first course in microeconomics. I do regard it as rather foolish to search for a lost watch under the lamppost if I know that is not where I lost it; and I do find myself rather impatient with defences of neoclassical economics, which, as we know, does not capture very much of the real world ("But, gee, however unrealistic it is, we can reason from it, we can draw strong, if incorrect, conclusions from it!"). In economics we must try to deal with a real world – the world of policy, the world of individual decisions – and I think we need to be quite careful that we are at least looking at the place where the watch is.

Now Friedman, of course, in his famous methodological essays has some things to say about this too. He had great praise for Galileo's theory of falling bodies; he did not complicate it with a lot of details like air resistance. At one point Friedman even says that theories are better, the more unrealistic they are. That is fine, but if I were manufacturing parachutes, I am sure I would not use the law of gravity without including a term for air resistance, otherwise the parachutes would not work very well. Basically we are interested in having a theory that will help us with our work in the world, and if that theory does not contain the critical phenomena then it is going to give us very bad advice.

Now you talked about how useless it would be to have a 1:1 map. It is true that it would cover the surface that it was mapping, but I would not worry about that. We do not yet have even a 1 in a million map, and so if we get it down to 1:150.000 or 1:20.000, I think we will be a great deal better off. When I hike in the mountains I like to have a map not much worse than 1:40.000, if I can get one, and then I feel I know the terrain I am on. So maybe a century from now someone can worry about whether we are learning too much about the economic system and whether our theories are too full of details, but it is not time yet for that worry.

I think that when we economists look at the history of science, we are too eager to look at physics, where you have these grand

29

laws like Newton's laws of motion. Physics has succeeded in finding a few laws that do many things. The laws are useful not because they are wrong in detail (as relativity theory and quantum mechanics have shown them to be), but because they work pretty well if you are not too small or do not move too fast. However if you are a solid state physicist who deals with materials, you find out that these laws do not go very far: you also need a lot of specific information about crystal structures and all sorts of things. You do not try to reason everything from Newton's three laws or even quantum mechanics without many auxiliary assumptions.

If we go to biology we find much more of the same. Biology, even modern molecular biology and modern evolutionary biology, is not governed by a few overarching laws. Biologists are accustomed to expending enormous labor collecting facts. They theorize about facts, but they do not theorize without facts. You do not get praise from biologists for theorizing without facts. I am not arguing that we should have no theories: bounded rationality is a theory. But there is much more to the theory than that phrase: namely, a great deal that we have learned about how to characterize human thinking and decision making. The question is whether economics is going to consist of its "three laws of motion" (always maximize utility subject to constraints), or whether it is going to have theories like those in biology, theories like those in solid state physics, theories like those in chemistry; whether economics, like those other sciences, is going to bring in an enormous number of very concrete facts. I am betting on the latter if we want a theory that does not keep us always under that lamppost where the watch is not.

Teaching elementary microeconomics to people who are not economists, and particularly to people who have had some experience of the business world, can be a rather unnerving experience for an economist, because students will often be dissatisfied with an abstract description that does not conform to the world that they know. I think they are right to be dissatisfied. Recently, I have been studying some of our current microeconomics textbooks, and asking myself what I would put in place of the fictions about global rationality – prior to the time when we will have the facts that we need, but given only the facts we know now and the theories of human thinking we have now. It turns out that most of the simple supply and demand theory of market equilibration can be taught without even mentioning utility maximization. As staunch a defender of utility maximization as Gary Becker said the same thing in an article he published in 1962 in the *Journal of Political Economy*. He said, for example, that the negative slope of the demand curve can be caused by much simpler things than utility maximization: in particular, by budget constraints.

If we went through that elementary microeconomic textbook and threw out most of the talk about utility maximization and the like, and left in it a lot of common sense about the fact that if there are very few houses on the market and lots of people who have money and want houses, that the prices for houses are going to go up – if we did that, we would keep most of the useful parts of that economic textbook without (I must be careful of my words now; I was going to say "fraudulently pretending") – without pretending that these realistic parts of the theory derive in some way or another from utility maximization. In general, they don't. Sooner or later there is going to be a textbook that will teach what is viable in price theory without that pretence of utility maximization.

A couple of books today on the American market try to play both sides of the game: they give a standard account, using utility maximization, in the first 16 chapters and then they add another four chapters showing how they really believe the system works. And when I asked the author of one of these books why he did that, he said, "Well, after all, we are publishing in a market". Perhaps the world is not ready for the books that leave out the maximizing chapters and only include the realistic ones. But it will be ready sooner or later; for that is the way the world really works.

SECOND LECTURE
The Role of Organizations in an Economy

1. Organizations and Markets. – 2. Altruism and Organizational Identification. – 3. Organization, Management, and the Economy. – 4. Conclusion.

My main goal in this second chapter will be to discuss the nature and operation of business organizations, or firms, and the place they must have in a theory of a modern economy. First, I will describe the place of the business firm in the economy, and in particular, the relations between firms and markets. Next, I will explore the goals and motivations of economic actors in organizational settings. This will call for a consideration of the role of altruism in human behavior, and the particular form of altruism that we call organizational loyalty, or identification. Finally, with the firm located in the economy, and with a sound motivational theory in hand, I will examine the operations of the firm, and the implications of its behavior for the economy.

1. Organizations and Markets

In the summer of 1988, I spent a delightful two weeks in a *certosa* near the city of Siena, participating in a workshop on the theory of the firm that had been organized by the Department of Economics of the University of Siena. Most of the papers that were presented lay within the framework of the so-called "New Institutional Economics", which provides the predominant view of the business firm in contemporary economic theory. In listening to the talks given by my colleagues, I was struck by the fact that the firm was almost always described in relation to the markets in which it participates: the market for products and raw materials, but especially the labor market and the terms on which its managers and workers were assumed to be employed. All sorts of elaborate explicit and implicit contractual arrangements were described to account for the fact that people who are employed

33

by firms often work toward the profit goals of their employers rather than pursuing their own self interest.

I have not stated the matter quite accurately. It was not that, in these descriptions of employment, the employees advanced the firm goals *in conflict* with their own interests, but that the employment contracts were shaped in such a clever, perhaps even Machiavellian, fashion, that the interest of the firm and self-interest were made to coincide – to a degree.

a. The Employment Relation

In an earlier period of my career, when I was a student of organizations rather than economics, the employment relation was described somewhat differently (Simon, 1951). The employee entered the firm, at whatever level, with the understanding that he or she would receive a salary or wage in return for a willingness to accept the authority of the organization. "Accepting authority" meant occupying the working hours in the activities that were defined and specified by the organization's system of authority, and carrying out these activities in a way that would promote the organization's goals (presumably profit) directly or indirectly.

Of course the employees did not sign a blank cheque. Presumably they would only be asked to do things that were consistent with an explicit or implicit job description, and with their abilities and skills. But, within this area, there would be a zone of acceptance and indifference, and so long as orders did not go beyond the limits of this zone, behavior would be determined by orders, legitimate organizational authority, rather than by the employees' preferences. This arrangement was advantageous to both employer and employees. It enabled the employer to decide, at any given time, what needed to be done and to ask someone to do it. It enabled the employees to receive compensation for devoting themselves to specific tasks where they had no strong preferences for doing one rather than another.

This latter picture of employment does not suggest that enforcement of the employment contract presents any great difficulties. The employees have no particular motive for not

34

doing what they are asked to do; there is no reason to expect that they will be slackers, leaving the work to someone else (the "public goods" problem), or that they will spend their time pursuing some private interest. In the *New Institutional Economics,* on the other hand (e. g., Williamson, 1975), the terms of contracts – the ways in which asymmetry of information and other factors affect these terms and the enforceability of contracts – are a central theme.

I will take up these motivational issues in the second part of my lecture, returning, for the moment, to the relation of the firm to markets. During the Siena lectures it occurred to me that, contrary to what I was hearing, the lives of most people in a modern industrial society are not spent mainly in markets, but in the interiors of individual firms. Eighty per cent or more of the working population is employed by firms, and only a small fraction of these have direct contact with the firms' markets to any significant extent. Their working lives are spent largely well inside the skin of the firm.

b. Full-bodied Organizations

It occurred to me also that any creature floating down to our Earth from Mars would perceive the developed regions to be covered mostly by firms, these firms connected by a network of communications and transactions that we know as markets. But the firms would be much more salient than the markets, sometimes growing, sometimes shrinking, sometimes dividing or even swallowing one another. Surely they would appear to be the active elements in the scene. How curious, in the light of this predominance of firms, that in economics we describe the firms as small skeletal structures embedded in the network of markets, rather than describing markets as threads that link robust firms.

These speculations have led me to consider how an organization-centric picture of the economy would differ from a market-centric picture (Simon, 1991). A major difference is that the real-world firm would have much more flesh on its bones than the firm of neoclassical economics. The latter is pretty much summed up

35

by a production function and an entrepreneur, who makes decisions by comparing costs of production with the prices at which the corresponding amounts of product could be sold. The system is almost all skin, in direct contact with the market.

The firm or organization theory is a quite different affair. It contains a complex system of behavior in its interior, and a large part of its management's time is spent in assuring that its vital organs are functioning properly. The design of products (and not just the choice of products) is often a central concern, and marketing procedures, manufacturing procedures, pricing policies, the central organization structure, even long-term strategies are designed, and not just chosen. Design calls for initiative, focus of attention on major problems, search for alternatives. One cannot choose the best, one cannot even satisfice, until one has alternatives to choose from.

Especially in the case of new or expanding firms, the entrepreneur does not face an abstract capital market. He or she exerts much effort to induce potential investors to share the company's views (often optimistic) about its prospects. This executive is much closer to Schumpeter's entrepreneur than to the entrepreneur of current neoclassical theory. Whether the firm expands or contracts is determined not just by how its customers respond to it, but by how insightful, sanguine and energetic its owners and managers are about its opportunities – by how much they possess of the "animal spirits" that Keynes was obliged to introduce into his account of the trade cycle (Nelson and Winter, 1982).

To a certain extent, but not within the formal theory, macroeconomics recognizes the existence of this full-bodied firm, for macrotheory today does incorporate executives' expectations about the future. But it has little to say about how such expectations are formed except when it claims, implausibly, that entrepreneurs carry around in their heads neoclassical models of the economic system, and thereby form their expectations "rationally".

Sometimes macroeconomics even introduces into its model of the firm the costs and returns from research and development activity, a recognition that decision making encompasses the design of products as well as choice among them. But it does not often face up to the question of how firms and their managers go about estimating those costs and returns – if, indeed, they do estimate them.

c. Interaction of Organizations with Markets

How do full-bodied organizations interact with markets? Von Hayek argued long ago (von Hayek, 1945) – and Adam Smith (1789) long before him – that "[the price system] enables entrepreneurs, by watching the movement of comparatively few prices, as an engineer watches the hands of a few dials, to adjust their activities to those of their fellows . . ." There is no talk here of optimization, only of "adjustment". So far, so good. Prices (*together with inventories or backlogs of orders*) do serve as crucial indicators for short-term adjustments. But when the adjustment is unsatisfactory for the longer run, they tell the entrepreneurs precious little about what to do about it. They are like inspections under a good system of quality control. They tell when the system is operating within control limits, not how to diagnose and fix it when it is not.

The common and understandable practice of pricing by marking up costs assures liquidity, at least in the short run, if only there is at least a modest base of fixed costs. The adjustment of production rates to sales holds price margins within a moderate range without excessive absorption of cash by inventories. All of this has little or nothing to do with the usual theorems of optimal pricing and production rates. A simple feedback of price, inventory and sales information adjusts production and prices and maintains a tolerable steady state over considerable intervals of time without any close calculation of margins or optima.

Nor does this self-adjusting system have much to do with the information that the firm must gather in order to carry out the numerous search and design activities mentioned earlier. A study of the allocation of management time would almost certainly show that it is the latter that account for most of the managers' days, not the effortless adjustment to price signals that von Hayek mentions.

In addition, neoclassical theory assumes that there are clear boundaries between the elements known as "firms". In practice these boundaries are highly ambigious: automobile dealerships, and manufacturers who have longstanding relations with regular suppliers exemplify one side of this ambiguity; corporate divisions of conglomerates, which have their own profit and loss statements and must live within their own resources, dealing with the corporate office as with an investment bank, exemplify the other side. A corporation together with its customary suppliers, or a conglomerate with its divisions, can – in close resemblance to a colony of algae – be viewed as one organism or a multitude.

Markets represent only a part, if an important part, of the channels of communication and coordination between organizations; but markets are also sometimes significant mechanisms of adjustment within single organizations. When we look at the organizations of the real world, we find much more structure and complexity than is hinted at in the theory of the firm, whether in its classical or its "new institutional" versions. I will return to these topics later, and a fuller picture of the business firm, after we have looked a little more closely at the problems of motivating appropriate executive and employee behavior within it. I turn to that question next.

2. Altruism and Organizational Identification

In the first chapter, I pointed out that the neoclassical theory of rational behavior is wholly neutral with respect to the content of the economic actor's utility function; but that as soon as the apparatus is applied to problems of the real world – whether the theory of the firm, or public choice or economic policy – this neutrality is abandoned, and replaced by the assumption that individuals seek specific things: usually wealth (or sometimes power). It is this latter assumption that has produced the theory of the firm espoused by the *New Institutional Economics* (Williamson, 1975).

Managers and employees, according to this theory, are selfish wealth-seekers, and they will direct their actions towards the maximization of the firm's profits only if that direction can be enforced by the shareholders (or by higher levels of management if the latter have also been held to the correct direction). If we make different assumptions about human motives, the whole situation shifts radically.

Suppose, for example, that managers and employees were altruistically inclined toward the firm: that they obtained utility from seeing it prosper. Then the intricate contracts of the New Institutional Economics would be superfluous. The mere act of employment would guarantee loyalty to the firm's goals without the need for detailed supervision of behavior, or concern for slacking off and cheating. But isn't this pure utopian moonshine? Does it call for even a moment's consideration?

a. Human Altruism and neo-Darwinian Theory

Let us look at the theory of altruistic behavior, first from a Darwinian standpoint, then in the context of social institutions like those in our own societies. The neo-Darwinian theory of evolution takes genetic fitness as its point of focus. Fitness means the number of progeny produced in a given period of time. If two individuals or groups are competing for occupancy of a single environmental niche, then the one with greater fitness will in time extinguish the other, the ratio of the fitter population to the less fit growing exponentially.

Neo-Darwinian theorists have argued that there is little room for altruism in this scheme, where altruism is defined to mean behavior that is beneficial to the fitness of other individuals, but costly to the actor. Altruists will lose out in the competition to other individuals who are otherwise identical but not altruistic. The arithmetic of the matter is simple. Let X be the "innate" fitness of each individual, bp the benefit for the recipient of altruism, where p is the percentage of altruists in the population, and c the cost of altruism. Then the fitness, F_s, of the selfish person will be:

$$F_s = X + b(c)p,$$

39

where b is a function of c, the amount of altruism; While the fitness, F_A, of the altruist will be less by c, the cost of altruism:

$$F_A = X\text{-}c\text{+}b(c)p.$$

If two persons share most of the same genes, then altruism of one toward the other will enhance the fitness of their common genes. Hence, the theory does not rule out altruism toward *close* relatives (i.e., siblings or children). Altruism towards more distant relatives has a doubtful prospect of surviving. There are a few other circumstances under which altruism is consistent with the neo-Darwinian apparatus, but they are rather esoteric, with little apparent relevance for the human species. But before we accept the verdict that altruism must be very rare, let us look at human behavior more closely. I will follow the argument of Simon (1990).

In the first chapter, I proposed that the major reason why we humans do not behave in a globally rational way was because we cannot. Our knowledge is exceedingly limited in comparison with the complexity of the situations in which we make our decisions; our ability to compute the consequences of our actions or to find the most effective actions is miniscule in comparison with the sizes of the problem spaces in which the search for an optimum must be carried out. We are creatures of bounded rationality.

A second salient characteristic of the human condition is that we are highly dependent on those around us – initially the family, later larger social groups – even for our survival, much less our production of progeny. Most of what we know, most of what we are able to do, is acquired from our social environments from the time of birth on into adulthood. Among the "facts" that we "know", or at least believe, there are very few that we have established ourselves on the basis of evidence that we have ourselves observed and reasoning that we have carried out.

We avoid cholesterol because our physician (or some other information source that we trust) has assured us that it is bad for our health, not because we have gathered or evaluated any biological evidence on the matter. Many of us count among the consequences of our actions their effect upon our prospects in a life after death, an evaluation that is obviously socially determined. We are highly susceptible to social influence and persuasion, a susceptibility that I will call *docility*. I use the term "docility" here in its sense of teachability or educatability, not in its alternative sense of passivity or meekness. Persons who are deficient in docility in the former sense do not usually survive very long. If they cannot learn at all, they are unlikely to reach adulthood. If they learn too little or slowly, or accept too little of what others seek to teach them, they will encounter innumerable difficulties and hazards, natural and social.

There is a close connection between bounded rationality and docility. If our computational abilities were unlimited, so that we could discover and carry out the choices mandated for the maximization of expected utility, then we would not need help from others. The farther the complexities of the real world extend beyond our capabilities for knowledge and calculation, the more valuable is docility, to enable us to benefit from the collective knowledge and skill of our society – Adam Smith's division of labor in a new guise.

Docility contributes enormously to our fitness, hence has been selected by the evolutionary process, because the things we are taught or are influenced to do are generally beneficial to us. This does not mean that all of them are beneficial. In a society of docile people, individuals can sometimes be directed toward behavior that benefits the society while harming the person who engages in it (e. g., jumping into a river or entering a burning building to rescue someone). As long as the "tax" imposed by such behaviors is not as great as the benefit from docility, docile people, who will now also exhibit altruism, will remain fitter than selfish non-docile people.

But why do docile people not learn to distinguish between the advice and information that is personally beneficial and that which is altruistic but harmful? The answer is that they cannot because of their bounded rationality. Very intelligent persons might be able to screen harmful advice more successfully than less intelligent persons, but they can still only evaluate independently a tiny part of the information and influence they receive. Do we really know that cholesterol is bad for us, or is this simply

41

a myth whose acceptance conveys some unknown benefit to other members of society? And if we feel confident on this one point, how about the other hundred thousand, or perhaps million, beliefs that we hold? Even for the most intelligent people, a substantial measure of docility, hence of susceptibility to the altruism "tax" imposed by society, will contribute to their fitness.

Acceptance of the social "tax" of altruism may be enforced by other mechanisms that have an evolutionary base, and that are themselves selected because they contribute to docility. Guilt appears to be one such mechanism, shame another. Even without these additional processes, the combination of bounded rationality with docility provides a powerful mechanism for the maintenance of a substantial level of altruistic behavior in human society.

This argument for the possibility of altruism can be formalized with only a simple alteration of our previous pair of equations. If we call d the gain in fitness derived from docility, and c the cost to fitness of the altruistic behavior that the docile person is "tricked" into, then the fitness of the non-docile person is:

$$F_A\text{-}(S) = X + b(c)p,$$

while the fitness of the altruistic, docile person is:

$$F_A\text{-}(A) = X + (d\text{-}c) + b(c)p.$$

As long as $d > c$, the altruistic, docile person will be fitter than the selfish, non-docile one. Since d is likely to be very large in relation to X, c, the tendency toward altruism, can also be strong.

Having shown that altruism, at least in the Darwinian sense, is likely to be prominent in behavior, it is time to look at the implications of this result for economics in general and for the theory of the firm in particular.

b. Altruism in Economics

Altruism generally denotes something quite different in economics than in evolutionary theory. In general utility theory, where the contents of the utility function are unspecified, it is almost impossible to define altruism. Whatever the rational actor chooses contributes to his or her utility, hence is not altruistic – by definition. As we saw in the first chapter, economic analysis does not often hold to this general theory, but in order to make predictions about behavior, replaces utility by wealth, or something similar, as the quantity to be maximized. But if we assume that wealth is the main or sole source of utility, altruism can now be defined in a wholly operational way. Any behavior that benefits another at the expense of the benefactor's wealth is now altruistic.

Under the conditions of modern societies, the connection between altruism as defined by neo-Darwinian theory, and altruism as defined by utility theory when wealth is the chief goal is tenuous at best. In fact, at least in first-world societies, there is a negative correlation between wealth and number of progeny, a correlation that would probably be maintained even if we had accurate information about illegitimate children! Hence any doubts about the possibility of maintaining altruistic behavior because of its possible harmful effects on fitness can be dismissed.

Whatever their connection with Darwinian fitness, both bounded rationality and docility are observably salient properties of the human species. Hence the mechanism to produce altruism by "taxing" docility, described in the previous section, remains effective in a world where utility is produced by wealth. In what ways does this altruism exhibit itself?

We have data on some modest manifestations of altruism. Americans, on average, give about two or three per cent of their income to charities that qualify for tax exemption, in addition to donating extensive amounts of personal time to voluntary activities. Public choice theory has pointed to other apparently altruistic activities that produce public goods and could be avoided by shirking: voting being a notable and important example.

c. Organizational Loyalty and Identification

But it is likely that the most extensive and important of all altruistic behaviors are those deriving from loyalty to the groups to which people belong, including family, city, nation, ethnic and religious groups – and organizations. We are so familiar with these loyalties that we hardly think of them as involving altruism.

We only have to look at the bitter ethnic struggles going on around the world today to see thousands of young men volunteering to undergo the hazards of war in support of a group loyalty.

Other expressions of group loyalty are generally less spectacular. We see a great many people working very hard toward group goals, the goals, for example, of the organizations in which they earn their livings. To be sure, organizations provide economic rewards for employment, and better, more devoted work, probably receives greater rewards, on average, than work that is poor in quality and minimal in quantity. But the reward systems of organizations are exceedingly imperfect, first because it is impossible to observe behavior in any continuous and comprehensive way; second because, for many jobs, especially the more responsible ones, it is impossible to measure the contribution (much less the marginal contribution) of an executive or other employee with any accuracy; and third, because competition between individuals and power struggles in organizations reduce substantially the correlation between rewards and contributions to organizational goals. For all of these reasons, the relation between contributions and rewards, short run or long run, cannot be very strong.

Shirking is possible on a large scale in organizations (and occurs at substantial levels). But everyone who has had experience with organizations knows that most employees, especially those whose work is intellectually and professionally challenging and not routine, devote themselves to the organization's goals far beyond the devotion required to avoid detection of their shirking. When we speak of an organization as having high morale, a principal criteria we have in mind is the loyalty and devotion of employees to the organization's goals.

Loyalty has not only a motivational component – internalization of the organizational goals – but also a cognitive component. By virtue of occupying a particular position in an organization, with responsibilities for particular subgoals and with a specialized environment of tasks and incoming information, an employee not only acquires the goals appropriate to the position but also represents his or her world with the position and its concerns at its focus, and attends mainly to information that is relevant to the focus (Simon, 1947). Here we see again the powerful influence of bounded rationality on behavior. Since a person can only be aware, at any given time, of a tiny corner of the world, that corner becomes the world, and indirect consequences that are not represented in it are largely ignored.

Because organizational attachments have this powerful cognitive component, as well as a motivational one, it is customary to speak of organizational *identification* rather than loyalty. The term identification subsumes both the motivational and the cognitive components of the attachment. It is not unknown for the manager of a division, promoted to headship of the department, to turn down a budget request submitted during his or her occupancy of the original position.

Point of view can, and usually does, change radically with organizational position. Sometimes we are very cynical about our organizations (especially governmental ones). We see only power struggles and inefficiency. We must keep in mind that the modern developed world has achieved very high levels of productivity with the aid of large-scale organizations, and would not know how to maintain that productivity without them.

The low productivity of Soviet Russia has usually been attributed, at least by economists, to its misguided attempt to supplant markets by central planning. This explanation does not account for the disintegration of the Russian economy after the liberalization of the regime. We should consider the hypothesis that failures in skills of organizing and in enlisting organizational loyalties play a major role in Russian economic difficulties today, and very likely played such a role long before *perestroika* began. Organizations are at least as large a part of the story of Russian disorganization and failure as are markets.

3. Organization, Management, and the Economy

We have now reached our first two objectives: of comparing the theory of the firm as it has appeared in economic theory with a different view of it that comes out of organization theory; and of examining the role of altruism (particularly in the form of organizational identification) in behavior within the firm. In the final portion of this chapter, I would like to say more about the ways in which firms operate and the conditions under which markets, privately owned firms, non-profit firms or government agencies are likely to work most satisfactorily.

a. The Choice Between Organizations and Markets

The central property of markets is that they direct resources to those uses in which they have the highest value. Under perfect competition, they lead to an equilibrium that is Pareto optimal. No shift from such an equilibrium can benefit all participants in the economy. To explain the existence of organizations, we must identify conditions in the real world that depart from these conditions of market optimality.

It might be supposed that the economic advantages of a division of labor are sufficient to explain why so much of an economy's work is done by organizations. But if we examine the famous passages in *The Wealth of Nations* on the advantages of a division of labor we find that specialization, by itself, does not imply a preference for organizations over markets. In Adam Smith's time, the factory system was in its very beginnings, and most of the examples he cites of the division of labor involve specialization among crafts or sub-crafts, without any assumption that the specialists need to be gathered together in a factory or organized by a company (Smith, 1789). Cottage industry and the putting-out system, not the factory, were the characteristic, market-oriented, ways of organizing production in the 18th Century. Something more than the division of labor is required to explain why these institutions were largely replaced by the factory system and large corporations in the two centuries that followed.

One way to approach this question is to examine the relative costs and benefits of an employment contract as compared with a contract to purchase goods and services. In making this comparison, the *New Institutional Economics* has emphasized, on the one hand, the transaction costs that are associated with contracting, and on the other hand, the costs and problems of enforcing the terms of contracts upon selfish individuals who, without such enforcement, would work toward their own interests rather than the interests of the other contracting party whenever the two sets of interests did not coincide (Williamson, 1975).

In a contract for goods or services, the product that is exchanged can be specified in a variety of ways. Typical contracts for complex machinery may specify the exact blueprint to be followed, the materials to be used, and the tolerances to be met, as well as price and time of delivery. In other cases, the contract may specify performance characteristics (wattage of a motor, operating temperature, energy efficiency, and so on), and leave to the supplier the exact means for meeting these performance standards. The ideal is to leave to the manufacturer as much leeway as possible to produce a desirable product at the lowest cost, at the same time avoiding acceptance of an inferior product through failure to bar cost-cutting that reduces quality. Methods of specifying a product vary from industry to industry, and change from one era to another. Steel, once specified in terms of alloy composition is now more often specified in terms of measures of strength, ductility, and so on. Legal and other professional services are commonly purchased by the hour.

A number of diverse factors are at work in determining mutually advantageous forms of contract: locus of technical expertise (in seller or buyer), adequacy of quality measurements, opportunities for cost saving without damage to product, chances that cost cutting will produce an inferior product, ease or difficulty of communicating requirements, and others. As the *New Institutional Economics* emphasizes, many of these factors relate to the possibility of the supplier pursuing private interest at the expense of the interest of the purchaser.

When we look at real-world contracting practices, we see that, even in the case of market transactions, far more communication than the simple exchange of price information takes place between the contracting parties. The individual firm needs to know a great deal about the environment surrounding it beyond the prices of raw materials and products. Particularly in the case of producers' goods, large volumes of detailed technical information (e.g., plans for a building) must be exchanged, and continuous

47

consultation must take place between technicians employed by the two parties. Much more information exchange is required than von Hayek's (1945) simple price signals. The greater the volume of this exchange, the more a purchasing arrangement begins to look like a collaboration between two divisions of a company. This is one major reason why the boundaries of firms become fuzzy and the make-or-buy decision is often not clear cut.

Under these circumstances, the enforceability of the employment contract – the degree to which employees can be expected to pursue company goals when these conflict to some extent with their own interests – becomes a central factor in determining the relative advantages of markets and organizations. To the extent that altruism, in the form of organizational identification, can be induced in employees, adherence to organizational goals can be assured to a higher degree than can be attained through close supervision. This is especially true for employees whose work is not routine but requires initiative in searching out problems and their solutions, or opportunities and the means for exploiting them – that is to say, most skilled, professional, and managerial employees. The capacity of people for identification with the organizations for which they work becomes a major force toward making organizations efficient systems for attaining goals, and effective competitors with markets.

The need for coordination is another force that pushes toward replacing markets with organizations. The term "coordination" can be very ambiguous. Setting up an organization unit to "coordinate" the activities of other units should usually be viewed as a danger signal that the problems of organization have not been thought through. The title of "Coordinator" does not communicate just what the bearer of the title is supposed to do.

I am going to use the term "coordination" in a narrower way: specifically, to speak of situations in which what is appropriate action for one individual depends on what another individual decides to do. In the competitive markets of the textbooks, coordination takes place automatically through price signals. But when someone is making parts of another's product, other considerations are involved: for example, the physical fit of the parts. "Coordinating" pistons with cylinders presents a problem of this kind. The invention of interchangeable parts through the specification of tolerances was an important advance that allowed division of work often to operate through markets without the need for organizational centralization.

But many requirements for coordination are not handled so easily. There may be several alternative ways to proceed, but it may be crucial that all parties to the activity proceed in compatible ways – that they all drive on the same side of the street, for example. Organizational authority is one mechanism for communicating to all the persons engaged in activities requiring coordination a set of common ground rules. The need for coordination, along with the possibility of creating organizational loyalties are perhaps two of the most important factors that give organizations an advantage over markets in many situations, and that account for the large role of organizations in the economic activity of a society like ours.

b. Private Ownership, Non-Profits, and Government Agencies

The plausibility of our analysis of the relative advantages of markets and organizations can be checked in a variety of ways by observing existing institutions. In those industries where private enterprise competes with government agencies (for example, water and power utilities, communications services), we can try to evaluate their relative efficiencies. A few such studies have been made, with largely inconclusive results. In some cases the private providers of services have appeared to be more efficient, in other cases the government providers. The evidence certainly provides no support for the claim that profit interests of owners are essential for efficiency. Evidently, comparable levels of efficiency can be attained with the help of internal economic rewards and organizational identifications.

In the United States, we have a great melange of universities, some supported by the States, some organized as non-profit institutions. Private corporations have not entered this industry, at least at elite levels (perhaps because of the governmental and charitable subsidies of the existing universities). As one who has spent all of his professional life in universities and paid a great

49

deal of attention to their management, I am unable to see any general superiority in the efficiency of non-profit over government-controlled universities, or vice versa. There are examples of superb, mediocre, and even deplorable institutions of both kinds.

Nor am I prepared to concede that universities generally operate at lower efficiencies than private corporations like General Motors or IBM. Of course it would not be easy to make this comparison in an objective way, especially since the extent to which universities achieve their stated objectives of educating students and creating significant new knowledge is not readily evaluated. So I will have to label my views on this comparison a conjecture rather than a verifiable fact.

In the recent discussions of the advantages of free market systems there has been considerable confusion between two independent variables: the form of ownership, and the centralization or decentralization of decision making. A free market system makes possible a considerable decentralization of decision making if not quite such a complete decentralization as von Hayek (1945) and other neoclassical economists have claimed. But the free market sends its signals to organizations quite independently of their form of ownership. A non-profit corporation that competes in a free market must float on its own bottom just as a profit-making corporation in that same market must. Each one can only spend the funds that it raises by providing services to its clients and inducing investment in its activities. The managers of a charitable organization are subject to the same discipline as the managers of the profit-making firm. If there is any difference it is only in the motives that lead individuals (e. g., donors of gifts to a college) to contribute resources.

The difficulty that has been experienced in finding any consistent relation between the forms of ownership of organizations and their operational efficiency is not wholly surprising, for direct participation in profits plays only a small role in motivating the loyalty of employees to business and other organizations. This is not to say that economic rewards are unimportant, but that they are seldom tied directly to profitability, and they are strongly reinforced by organizational identification.

Separating the question of form of ownership from the question of central planning is essential if we are to think clearly about the problems of national economic organization that are confronting many countries in the world today, and most notably, the now autonomous former components of the Soviet Union. That centralized national planning has performed badly is clear enough. Markets appear to be the only effective mechanisms we know for coordinating activities across an economy – that is, markets within a broader framework of governmental economic policy. But in the transfer from centralized planning to a market economy it is not obvious to what extent the production organizations need to be privatized, and there are many alternative possibilities. But to pursue this line of inquiry would take us too far from the central theme of this book.

4. Conclusion

In this chapter I have sought to sketch out a theory of the firm for a world in which most activities take place inside organizations, even though these organizations are linked by a network of markets. The neoclassical theory of the firm, which provides only a caricature of real firms, is wholly inadequate for this purpose.

First, we must recognize that choosing among a fixed set of alternative actions – and these mainly limited to the quantities of various products that will be produced – constitutes only a small, and relatively uninteresting part of the decision-making task within firms. Business managements are mainly occupied with a wide range of what I have called design tasks – design of products and of strategies for marketing, finance, manufacturing, and so on – and the success of a business depends largely on how well these tasks are performed.

Second, businesses are strongly oriented toward profit (or, in the case of non-profit organizations, toward matching costs with revenues), not because most of their employees receive economic rewards that are closely related to profits (they don't), but because executives and other employees become closely identified with the organization goals. Organizational identification is best interpreted as a form of altruism, and, in this chapter, I described the mechanisms, based firmly on human docility and bounded rationality, that produce altruism in general and organizational identification as an important species of it.

Third, while market mechanisms do facilitate decentralization of decision making in the economy, businesses exchange vastly more information than simply information about prices. The kinds and amounts of communication required by different organizational arrangements are major determinants of whether these arrangements will take the form of contracts to buy and sell or employment contracts, hence major determinants of the sizes and boundaries of business firms.

Fourth, organizations may have special advantages over markets as devices for coordinating activities where the actions that will be appropriate for one actor depend closely upon what other actors will do. Two major motives for bringing the production of goods and services together in an organization are to achieve this kind of coordination and to take advantage of the efficiencies derivable from organizational identifications, and the consequent commitment of participants to a common goal.

Fifth, in considering what arrangements in a society are likely to be most conducive to productive efficiency, the question of ownership must be separated from the question of centralization and decentralization. There is little, if any, evidence that nonprofit corporations, or government agencies – provided that they are subjected equally in both cases to the discipline of living within the revenues they can raise – behave in noticeably different ways.

The topic of organizations is a large one, and I have not attempted to deal with all, or even most, of its aspects in this chapter. I have focused on those issues that are, I believe, of most interest and relevance to economists, in particular, on the relations between organizations and markets. To handle these topics adequately, economics cannot get along with a theory of skeletal firms, amounting to little more than production functions; a full-bodied theory of organizations is required if we are to understand how economies really operate.

REFERENCES

von Hayek F. A., The use of knowledge in society, *American Economic Review*, 35, 1945, pp. 519-530.

Nelson R. and S. Winter, *An evolutionary theory of economic change*, Cambridge MA: Harvard University Press, 1982.

Simon H. A., *Administrative behavior*, New York: Macmillan, 1947.

Simon H. A., A formal theory of the employment relationship, *Econometrica*, 19, 1951, pp. 295-305.

Simon H. A., A mechanism for social selection and successful altruism, *Science*, 250, 1990, pp. 1665-1668.

Simon H. A., Organizations and markets, *Journal of Economic Perspectives*, 3, 1991, pp. 25-44.

Smith A., *The wealth of nations*, 5th edition, New York: The Modern Library, 1789 [1937].

Williamson O., *Markets and hierarchies*, New York: Macmillan, 1975.

DEBATE OF THE SECOND LECTURE
Interventions by Anna Grandori, Andrea Ichino,
Robin Marris, Daniele Terlizzese and others.

QUESTION. Is it a relevant phenomenon that altruism within a group is often hostility toward larger groups? I would like to hear a little more about that.

SIMON. In my own thinking I became concerned with the issue of altruism because neo-Darwinian arguments criticized the idea that anything except self-interest could be at work in the economic scene. I thought it was important that I understand what the argument was against altruism in this theory. Before I was done with my enquiry I had seen that altruism defined in Darwinian terms is very different from altruism as we define it in an everyday way. We do frequently refer to our attachment to groups as a sort of enlargement of the self, and that is reflected in the fact that we use the first person to refer to the group, "we". We also see that altruism often involves what we may call "organizational motives". Moreover, in many cases where there are conflicts of interest or supposed conflicts of interest between the group we call "we" and the group we call "they", we not only are willing to be very protective of the "we", but we are also willing to be very aggressive against "they". One way, at least, of writing the history of the human species and even of human civilization is as a series of aggressions of the "we" against the "they".

In history, our species does not always appear in a very pleasant light when we look at the extent to which a group that has a high level of group identification is willing to disregard or be hostile to the interests of people outside of that group. In history this is a very commonly observed aspect of human behavior, and we have to understand how it comes about. Now I suggested in my talk that the loyalty we exhibit to business organizations, although it doesn't usually take the form of cutting throats, does lead us into various kind, of competitive behaviors. Such behaviors are bad or good, depending on the arena in which they are

54

exhibited and what the rules of the game are. So I can agree fully with you that human beings, as they exhibit loyalty, do think of the "we" as somehow an extension of themselves and certainly behave as though it were an extension of themselves.

For example you can get the citizens of my city of Pittsburgh to vote for a bond issue which they will have to repay so that the Pittsburgh Pirates, our local baseball team, will not move to another city. They say: "We would lose the baseball team". Well, who would lose it? Some people would have to listen to the radio instead of going to the field, but most of them do not go often to the field anyway, which is why the team has economic problems. But because we identify with Pittsburgh, we suppose that if something is good for the Pittsburgh Pirates then it is good for us. This is a prominent aspect of human behavior and I agree with your characterization of it.

Business organizations and universities, and places of these sorts, illustrate the societal advantages to be gained from group loyalty, for it is essential to their operation and success. The kinds of things that are going on in many tortured countries today, with their ethnic wars, exhibit the unfortunate aspect of group loyalty. The mechanism underlying the behavior is the same in both cases, the goals to which it is directed are rather different.

QUESTION. I just wonder whether you could state what you think is to be demanded by theory; that is, when do you accept a theory as explanation of a collected set of facts?

SIMON. Let me try a relatively simple answer to that, but it is not a simple question, as you well know. We want theories for two purposes: (1) We human beings are curious about the world, we want to know how it works, and for that purpose we want our theories to be as good, as accurate, as predictive, as descriptive of the real world as we can make them, no holds barred. You can get curious about anything and try to construct a theory of it, as people frequently do. (2) On the other hand, we especially want theories because they may help us get on with our business in the world and achieve our various human goals. Economics has always been a science interested in explaining economic phenomena, but it is also a very practical applied field that wants to have something useful to say about how to manage a firm and something useful to say about how to manage an economy (or about whether you can manage an economy, as some people would prefer to put it).

I don't think that at any given moment of time we can get away without a theory. Keynes had something to say about that too; he said that when we imagine we are not following a theory we are probably following the words of some ancient madmen. These were not his exact words but they express his general intent. So, if we make decisions as we face the world, we are always operating within the context of some theory. Maybe it is a very naive theory, a trivial theory, a very low level theory or a much more exalted one. That is one dimension: how general and abstract is it? Another dimension is: how true is it?

In my lectures I have been emphasizing the need for economic theories that fit the facts, at least down to the level of detail that matters for policy. If I look around at those of my economist friends and colleagues who do a lot more than I do in macroeconomics and general economic policy, I see great differences of opinion even among people who are working primarily within the neoclassical framework. From this I gain the very strong suspicion that I expressed in my lecture: that a large part of their reasoning is not coming just from their theories, but also from all sorts of auxiliary assumptions they have to make along the way; because the theories by themselves will not explain the phenomenon. For example, modern utility theory without some specification of what is inside the utility function provides little or no guidance for economic policy of any kind. Before we do much with that theory we begin to talk about GNP and many other very specific assumptions about the content of the utility functions. Therefore, we have to be willing to carry the theory down to a level where it answers the kinds of questions we want to answer: policy questions if these are what we are trying to answer. I argued in my lecture that neoclassical theory does not do this and cannot do it without establishing a wide variety of facts (we often call them auxiliary assumptions) that have to be there before you can apply it to concrete situations.

QUESTION. I thought one of your methodological teachings was to try to discover hidden forms (maybe weak) of rationality behind behavior. Therefore, I would have expected a sort of enquiring of what kind of rationality can be hidden behind altruistic behaviors. To say that people are selected for their loyalty or for docility seems to point to an over-socialized concept of man. Can you clarify?

SIMON. There are several threads here. First, to have a theory of organizations you need not only a theory of how people reason about things but also a theory of what goals they are trying to accomplish when they are in organizations; you have to have a theory of motivations. That is true for rationality in general. Because rationality has to do with finding means to your ends, it must include some theory of the ends as well as the means, or at least of how the ends, as well as the means, are formed. Now, if you look at the economic literature on organizations, both the classical theory of the firm (profit maximization, using the production function as the underlying machinery), and the new institutional economics, you will see that it assumes pretty thoroughly throughout that the goals to which the rationality is directed, the things you reason about, are economic goals. That leads to a puzzlement (to which the new institutional economists have applied large efforts) as to why most people who work for organizations do anything that is particularly useful to the organization, in the light of the difficulties that I mentioned of evaluating their marginal product and the difficulty of supervising their work. How do organizations ever manage to get anything useful done, given those two very severe limitations?

Hence, we have to look for other motivations, and for a very long time I have been proposing some – since I wrote *Administrative Behavior*, more than 50 years ago. (I do not like to admit that because it shows that I never change my mind or learn: I am not docile.) In that book you will find a chapter on organizational identification or loyalty, which is presented as a very central characteristic of organizations (perhaps a little less central than I now think it to be). It seems to me essential that one understands correctly what the motivations are of people in

57

organizations, in order to understand how they exercise their rationality in business.

Now why the social Darwinism? It is not really social Darwinism, it is the standard variety of individualistic neo-Darwinism. I asked myself whether you could justify the assumption of organizational loyalty if biological mechanisms worked on people to select them for fitness, and whether any case at all could be made for anything except some form of very narrow selfishness in human behavior. The latter is usually assumed implicitly in most economic analysis, so that got me into the question of what kind of justification we could give for organizational loyalty.

I do not know whether my theoretical proposal leads to over-socialization or under-socialization. It certainly does not imply that people are totally docile; we all draw lines at certain points and exhibit scepticism at certain points about things that we have been told are for our own good, or for society's good. As I carried through this analysis, I began to see really how close, in terms of bounded rationality and docility, organizational loyalties are to all sorts of other group loyalties, and I became increasingly impressed with the role that these loyalties play in human behavior.

To make a moral judgement on this, I can see all sorts of cases where group loyalties produce over-socialized behavior; and we can look at the whole history of our century as exhibiting more examples than we would like to count of such behaviors. Certainly the number of contemporary examples is painfully large. So I do not want to make a moral case for organizational loyalty, but I do want to argue for its empirical, in-fact power. I did not have time in my talk to discuss its cognitive aspects, which also relate to bounded rationality. But the combined power of bounded rationality and organizational loyalties accounts for a large part of the efficiency of large organizations.

QUESTION. Differently from the previous intervention, I think that there is no contradiction between selection of altruists (or docile people) and rationality of altruism. The latter pertains to lower level of workers (for which altruism is largely internalized in the organization), while the former applies to high and middle management. Can you comment on that?

SIMON. I would agree very much that there are differences in degree of loyalty as we move down an organization, although sometimes I am more impressed by the extent of non-alienation of people at lower levels of the organization than I am with the extent of their alienation. It is true that almost all studies that have examined this have found that there is a direct correlation between alienation and size of organization, but alienation often takes the form, even in very large organizations, of loyalties to sub-organizations below.

The only other comment I would make is that there is a real public goods problem at the top. All executives can see that they succeed when the organization succeeds. That is true, but there are two ways of succeeding: succeeding by working and succeeding by loafing while others are working. We have to explain not merely the fact that people in successful organizations by and large get rewarded for the success of the organization, but we have to explain also why they do not treat that reward as a public good to which they do not have to contribute. We have a voting paradox here unless we can explain why they put their shoulders to the wheel.

THIRD LECTURE
Empirical Evidence for Economics

1. How Much Theory, and How Concrete? – 2. Implications of Data for Theory. – 3. The Sources of Data on Economic Processes. – 4. Seeking Empirical Data Outside the Business Firm. – 5. Decision Making in the Business Firm: Case Studies. – 6. Economic History. – 7. Data from "Applied" Economics. – 8. Survey Techniques. – 9. Conclusion.

The previous two chapters pointed to deep problems in contemporary neoclassical economics – problems in the conceptualization of rationality, and problems in characterizing business firms and their role in the economy. Positive changes were suggested in economic theory that would bring about a closer alignment of the theory with the conditions of the real world of trade and business. However, to bind economics to the facts of the world, as every empirical science must be bound, it is not enough to announce theories; they must be tested. In this third chapter, I will discuss the prospects for a better empirical grounding of economic theory, and the research methods available to us for achieving that grounding.

1. How Much Theory, and How Concrete?

Whatever the scientific domain we are concerned with, theory always falls short of describing reality in all of its detail. As has often been pointed out, perhaps most eloquently by Milton Friedman (1953), one of the virtues of a good theory is that it abstracts from reality, picking out and retaining just those features that are important and that should be retained in our focus of attention.

But it is hard to agree with one extension of that claim: that "unreality" of a theory is a positive virtue. When Galileo ignored air pressure in his law of falling bodies, he implicitly limited application of the law to situations where the missing term would not invalidate it. We would not recommend the law, in its simplified form, to parachute manufacturers, nor, I believe, would he. The correct statement about abstraction is that it is useful to abstract a theory by omitting those features that do not significantly affect the conclusions drawn from it in the domain to which it will be applied. Milton Friedman was careful to include this qualification when he made his celebrated defence of unreality, but it has sometimes been forgotten by economists who have followed him. When we criticize theories and when we build new ones we must take into account the uses we intend to make of them.

a. The Uses of Economic Theory

We can distinguish at least three uses of economics. First, we are interested in economic phenomena because of the same intellectual curiosity that attracts us to physical, or biological, or social phenomena in general. We need make no apology for curiosity about the world we inhabit; it is one of humankind's more admirable traits.

In the course of satisfying our curiosity, any phenomenon whatsoever is a fair target. We may wish to develop and employ the whole gamut of theory, from the most detailed and exact to the most abstract and general. Thus, there is every reason for us, in the pursuit of knowledge, to want a theory of rationality that tells us exactly how human beings reach judgments and make choices, and not just one limited to painting a highly abstract picture of these processes – and especially, not just one that paints a largely imaginative and unreal picture. For the same reason, we might want a detailed and, veridical theory of the behavior of people in business firms and other organizations.

A second reason we want economic theories is to help guide the actual management and operation of firms. The traditional theory of the firm treated mainly the relations of firms with markets and not the management of firms. The subdiscipline called "industrial organization" came a little closer, but not much. This gap in economic theory has been partially closed by the appearance of operations research (or management science), organization theory and artificial intelligence (expert systems).

If we are managers, or if we are giving advice to managers, we need a theory of firms that encompasses a great deal of detail about their operation. And it must be a theory that describes them realistically, not an "as if" theory. In both its descriptive and its normative aspects, it must describe, and prescribe for, the decision making processes of managers with close attention to the kinds of knowledge that are attainable and the kinds of computations that can actually be carried out.

A third use of economic theory, to understand and guide the operation of the economy, is the most venerable use, and still perhaps the one of greatest interest to most economists. It is not clear how detailed a theory of decision making or of business management we need for political economy. We need to retain those features of theory that make a difference, and discard those that do not. We need also to avoid features in our abstracted theories that will lead us to *wrong* conclusions at the macro level. (I will presently argue that we need a theory rather different from, and far more concrete than, received neoclassical doctrine.)

All of this would seem to be the most obvious common sense. What conclusions follow from such common sense? The principal conclusion is that achieving the three goals outlined above requires building an adequate, empirically based, theory of bounded rationality – that is, of procedural rationality – and applying the theory systematically to phenomena at both micro and macro levels. The knowledge that economic actors possess and do not possess, the computations that economic actors can make and cannot make must not enter economic theory as ad hoc assumptions, arrived at subjectively and without the discipline of systematic method. They must be shaped and tested by the sharpest empirical methods that we can devise.

2. Implications of Data for Theory

Discussions of methodology can be rather uninteresting unless some indication is given of the applications to which they can lead. Before I discuss the empirical methods available for strengthening our understanding of bounded rationality, I would like to offer some samples of changes in theory that data of these kinds can produce.

a. Organizational Identifications in the Firm

My first example comes from a very simple study that DeWitt Dearborn and I carried out in 1958, which produced results beyond our expectations. A group of 23 executives enrolled in an executive training program were asked to read a typical business policy case about the situation of a real firm (whose name was disguised). In their own companies, the executives represented different functions: 6 were in sales positions, 5 in production, 4 in accounting, 2 in a legal department, 2 in R&D, and one each in public relations, industrial relations, a medical department and purchasing. Before they discussed the policy case, they were asked to write down what they considered to be the most important problem facing the company described in the case.

Most of the sales executives (83%), but only 29% of the others mentioned marketing, sales, or distribution as the most important problem facing the company. Most of the production executives (80%), but only 22% of the others, mentioned internal organization as the most important problem. The industrial relations, public relations and medical executives, and no others, mentioned human relations as most important. Here is a vivid demonstration of how strongly identifications with particular functions, identifications shaped by particular professional training and by organizational experiences and responsibilities, focus attention on some phenomena and away from others. In a world in which not all problems can be at the head of the agenda simultaneously, these data say a great deal about how priorities are established, and how they shape policy.

There are some historical data, and many anecdotes, on the effect of the professional and organizational backgrounds of CEOs upon company policies. From our very simple study, we see another way of obtaining systematic data on these matters that can illuminate our theories of organizational decision making.

64

b. The Sizes of Business Firms

The neoclassical literature, including popular textbooks, provides a standard account of what determines the sizes of business firms. This account is purely deductive, based on the assumptions that companies have U-shaped short-run and long-run cost curves. In the short run, it states, the minimum of the short-run curve determines the level of production at which the company can operate at lowest cost. In the long run, by building new plants, the company can select any of these short-run alternatives; hence its long-run cost function is simply the envelope of the whole set of short-run functions.

Unfortunately, from this theory one cannot draw any conclusions about the size distribution of business firms in an industry or in the economy as a whole. If we assume that all companies have the same cost functions, at least in the long run, we would have to predict near-uniformity in company size, which is egregiously contrary to fact. If each company has a different cost function, then the size distribution depends on what the distribution of cost functions happens to be, and is not predicted at all by the theory.

On the other hand, if we start from the facts without strong theoretical presuppositions, we can find a rather straightforward explanation for the strong regularities that are observed. The actual distributions, whether for the industry or for the economy, are almost always well approximated by a Pareto distribution: a very skewed distribution that is similar to the log normal distribution, but with an even longer upper tail (Ijiri and Simon, 1977). Graphed on log-paper, the Pareto distribution appears as a straight line. But it is well known that this distribution can be generated by a stochastic process using the Gibrat assumption: the assumption that the expected rate of growth of each firm is proportional to the size it has already attained. Of course different firms may grow at widely different rates; the assumption is applied only to the average.

I say that these facts have a reasonable explanation because the opportunities for a firm to grow depend, in many ways, directly upon its current size: the amount of money it is able to borrow for new investment, the size of its marketing apparatus, its ability to increase production within the limits of current facilities, the rate at which it can increase its labor and supervisory forces without sacrifice of quality, and so on. With respect to each of these variables it is reasonable to assume that the limits (or costs) of growth will be approximately proportional to current size.

So the explanation that best fits the facts is that the changes in the sizes of firms are a function of many factors, probably both external to them (e. g., changes in markets) and internal (e. g., effectiveness of management, introduction of new products, and so on), but that current size is the most important determinant of the rate at which they can respond to changes in these factors by growing or shrinking. Growth is a stochastic process that can be explained, in the case of any given firm, only by detailed examination of the external and internal conditions affecting it. Because of the multiplicity of causal factors, the process will appear, from the outside, to be stochastic, and the actual data reflect this fact.

Further study of the empirical facts shows that if a firm experiences a more than average rate of growth at a particular time, it will likely regress fairly rapidly to the average. In one study of American data, Ijiri and Simon (1977, p. 181) found that a firm that doubled its share of the market in an initial four-year spurt of growth could expect, on average, to increase its share by only 28 per cent in the next four-year period.

All of these regularities can be observed and interpreted provided that we do not blind our senses by applying too quickly and mechanically the neoclassical apparatus, with its assumptions of global rationality, and its indifference to the boundedness of human rationality, including the rationality of managers and their vulnerability to unpredictable or unpredicted events.

Of course unpredictability, whether due to lack of reliable data, inadequacy of theories, or limitations on computational capabilities is at the very heart of bounded rationality. Meteorological prediction is as subject to it as is economic prediction.

c. The Compensation of Executives

The neoclassical explanation for differences in the levels of compensation of the executives of different firms again fails to provide an explanation for the observed distributions of salaries unless one makes very special (and empirically unsubstantiated) assumptions about the distribution of executive abilities. The facts are that compensation rises, on average, proportionately with the logarithm of company size, for chief executives, or the size of the organizational unit supervised, for other executives (Roberts, 1959).

Again, if we start from two institutional facts that can be gleaned from the descriptive literature on business organizations, we obtain a ready explanation of the logarithmic distribution. The first institutional fact is that organizations are hierarchical in shape, with a span of control (number of subordinates supervised directly by each supervisor) that generally lies within the limits of 5 to 15, and does not vary much from one level to another in the organization. The second institutional fact is that there are widely shared beliefs about the "fair" ratio of the supervisor's compensation to the compensation of his direct subordinates. Combining these two institutional facts leads, by simple mathematics, to the logarithmic relation between the salaries of executives and the sizes of the organizations they direct (Simon, 1957).

d. Implications for Normative Theory

Modern business schools teach economic theory and its offshoots – operations research, management science and expert systems – with the expectation that these will serve as useful tools for their graduates in making management decisions. A tool can be useful only if it fits human hands, human muscles, the human brain.

Consider, for example, linear programming, which has found many industrial uses, from the selection of most profitable petroleum blends in oil refineries to the selection of most economical feeds for beef cattle. The sharp blade of linear programming can be applied when: (1) the decision problem can be simplified, without too much loss of reality, in such a way that the quantity to be optimized can be expressed as a convex function of numerical variables, and the relations and constraints that characterize the situation can be expressed as linear equalities and inequalities; (2) data are available, in sufficiently close approximation to their real values, for estimating all of the parameters of the model; and (3) computational means are available for finding the problem solution at a reasonable cost and within a reasonable time.

These requirements place strong restrictions on the range of decision problems that can be aided by linear programming. Today, we rely on fast computers to relax computational restrictions, but it is not hard to find practical industrial problems – for example, typical factory scheduling problems – that lie well outside the range of the capabilities of present or prospective computers. Perhaps even more restricting are the requirements of most management decision tools that all the information about the problem be statable, at least to an adequate approximation, in numerical form.

New tools, especially the technology of expert systems and other techniques derived from artificial intelligence, are widening greatly the range of decisions that can be assisted by computers. Many expert systems are designed to seek satisfactory (satisficing) solutions instead of optimizing solutions, thereby making it feasible to handle many kinds of decisions whose optimal solutions are computationally unobtainable. Artificial intelligence systems are also able to handle information in verbal, and even pictorial or diagrammatic, form as readily as numerical information. They thereby permit the extension of management decision aids into domains that are qualitative rather than quantitative in nature.

The new tools coming from artificial intelligence research are heavily influenced by the premise that human problem solving, especially in poorly structured domains, depends mainly on selective (heuristic) search among possibilities, and that in practice, satisfactory solutions can often be found when optimal solutions cannot. Because artificial intelligence must be preoccupied with computational feasibility (for people or computers), the premises of bounded rationality are built into its foundations.

Artificial intelligence methods are fully compatible with economic theory based on bounded rationality; in general, they are not compatible with neoclassical theory, with its assumptions of global rationality and its indifference to questions of whether solutions can be found with available computational means.

e. Strong versus Weak Assumptions

Artificial intelligence tools incorporate assumptions of rationality (they would not be useful for normative purposes if they didn't), but a rationality suitable to human beings. Therefore, there is an excellent prospect that they can be of great utility in constructing descriptive, as well as normative, theories for economics. As a first step, we need only substitute satisficing assumptions for optimizing assumptions in our typical economic analyses of the behavior of firms and markets to see whether our theories are still strong enough to reach useful conclusions.

As one familiar example, it has been known for a long time that the fact that demand curves generally have negative slopes can be derived directly from budget limitations, without any appeal to equating marginal utilities (Becker, 1962). If the price of a commodity rises while incomes do not, consumers will have to cut their purchases of that commodity or others.

For similar reasons, we do not have to invoke profit maximization to explain why suppliers will cut prices or (even more frequently) reduce output when inventories are accumulating at current prices. Simple satisficing feedback mechanisms will behave in this way, without assuming that anything is being optimized, and without requiring the kinds of information that would have to be provided, or the kinds of computations that would have to be carried out to implement genuine optimization. The only rationality that is required is the common sense that, for reasons of lack of space, working capital limits, or what not, inventories can't be allowed to accumulate indefinitely, and accumulation can be halted either by reducing production or by depending on a negatively, sloped demand curve to increase sales when price is lowered.

Occam's Razor, as well as what is known empirically about

human decision processes, argue for the more parsimonious, satisficing, theory, which reaches these conclusions without unrealistic assumptions about human behavior, over the supposititious utility maximizing theory. But parsimony is not the only reason for preferring the simpler and more realistic course. Unnecessarily strong assumptions, like those of optimization, allow correspondingly strong conclusions to be drawn (for example, about the amounts of inventories that will actually be held). And there is no reason to suppose that these surplus conclusions, depending as they do upon unrealistic premises, will describe the real world.

The models of a satisficing theory would make us skeptical of claims that markets produce Pareto efficiency. The usefulness of markets in an economy does not hinge on their operating at close to perfect efficiency, and Adam Smith's powerful advocacy of free markets did not depend on any such assumption. His practical realism is always expressing itself: "But market price may be kept above natural for a long time, in consequence of want of general knowledge of high profits, or in consequence of secrets in manufactures, which may operate for long periods, or in consequence of scarcity of peculiar soils, which may continue for ever. (pp. 59-61, marginal heads)".

Similarly the unworldly conclusion that markets must equilibrate with full employment of resources would not follow from a satisficing theory. In the first chapter I observed that when Keynes (or Marshall or Lucas, for that matter) wished to introduce the possibility of unemployment, their first step was to replace the global rationality of one or more of the economic actors with bounded rationality. Labor, or businessmen, as the case may be, were suddenly assumed to be suffering from a money illusion. It was precisely these kinds of departures from perfect rationality, not neoclassical optimization theory, that were required to account for the phenomena.

3. The Sources of Data on Economic Processes

The most important data that could lead us to an understanding of economic processes and to empirically sound theories of them reside inside human minds. We are accustomed to thinking of economics in terms of transactions in which money is exchanged for goods or services, or of manufacturing processes that produce and consume products, or of shipments of goods from one part of the globe to another. But if we are interested in the causes of these events, we must seek to discover what went on in the heads of those who made the relevant decisions. Neoclassical economics is right in finding the core of its subject in the act of rational decision; its deficiencies arise from failure to ascertain how decisions are actually taken. And to ascertain that, we need to know about processes that occur within heads.

We have seen that the principal kinds of data available to Adam Smith were his own experiences, his ability to empathize with people placed in various situations, and a miscellany of published anecdotes and historical accounts of economic institutions and events. There were a few, very few, quantitative data available to him. Most of these concerned prices. Occasionally, he himself made calculations of the productivity increases achieved by new technology. (See, for example, his calculation [A. Smith, 1989, page 18], of the efficiences of water over road transportation.)

We find some similar examples of appeals to empirical evidence scattered through Marshall's *Principles*, but although substantially more quantitative data were available to Marshall than to Smith, statistics of money and prices were still at the center of the stage.

4. Seeking Empirical Data Outside the Business Firm

We will examine the many sources from which economists can obtain data to help build and test their theories. In the next section we will begin with several methods of empirical research that make use of publicly available data, or data that can be obtained in the laboratory. Neither of these methods requires contact with the economic actors, in markets or in business firms. In a second section, we will discuss research that goes inside the business firm for its data; and, in a third section, research that goes to individual economic actors, consumers or investors, say, for information about their choices, expectations or intentions.

a. Econometrics

Today, we have vast quantities of statistical information about production and consumption of goods and services, prices in security and commodity markets, incomes, taxes – virtually all of the externally visible products of production and trading activity. The accounting statements of publicly held corporations are available, sometimes at a level of considerable detail. These data derive from a host of governmental and private sources, and generally, their quality is as good as the nature of the raw source data will allow.

While all economists are gratified at the rich assortment of data now available, as contrasted with the austerity that confronted Adam Smith, and even Alfred Marshall, we are well aware that the information we possess still falls far short of what we need to construct and test our theories.

The difficulties we face fall into several categories. First, many of the data are very noisy, certainly by the standards of the physical sciences, and we must exert much energy to separate, even imperfectly, signal from noise. Even the total population of the United States is known only to an accuracy of a few per cent, and in the case of measures like national income, exports or imports, employment – the list is endless – the case is even worse. Since we are often interested in changes in these quantities, (e.g., whether income is up or down this month as compared with last month, even small errors in the aggregate quantities make short-run changes exceedingly difficult to assess. (Of course it is sometimes easier to measure changes in quantities than the quantities themselves.)

A second difficulty, especially as we move toward macroeconomics and political economy, is that we must combine our data into aggregates, with all of the pitfalls that are pointed out to us by the theory of aggregation. Our theories attempt to deal with such treacherous concepts as "the price level", "the level of employment", and "grain production", where different sampling and aggregation procedures can change our measures significantly. It has more than once been pointed out that the concept of a production function for the economy, or even for an industry, is a difficult, or even illusory, notion.

The matter is even worse with a concept like "the quantity of money", where we find, when we seek a rigorous definition, that the quantity of money is not something tangible, measurable against the standard kilogram in Paris, but a state of mind – more accurately, a composite state of innumerable minds of people who are forming expectations about the future and borrowing or lending, repaying debts or requesting their debtors to repay, on the basis of these expectations.

Our theories, then, and the models in which we express them, are constituted of these aggregated quantities, tied together by hypothesized relations that are also aggregated and approximate. The problem of stating these relations in a form that casts light on underlying mechanisms is the classical identification problem, so clearly illuminated nearly a half century ago by the work of Haavelmo, Koopmans and others (Koopmans, 1950; Hood and Koopmans, 1953). From the theory of identification we know that most theoretical models in economics contain far more empirical parameters to be estimated than equations to restrict their values. And if we are to estimate the parameters, and to test our theories, additional restrictions must be added in some way.

These restrictions (identifying assumptions) must come from our prior knowledge of the world, independently of the data we are using for our estimation. They are, in a strict sense, Bayesian priors, representing everything we knew about the world before we undertook the particular study whose model we are estimating and testing. The less certain our prior knowledge, the more alternatives we have in choosing our structural equations, with the consequent likelihood that there will be many conflicting interpretations of the data. It is for this reason that the same data can so often be used to "verify" the theory of rational expectations or to "refute" it.

Sixty years of extensive research in econometrics and the statistical theories associated with it have brought our techniques for analysing quantitative data to a high level of sophistication without giving us any reason to believe that these techniques will allow us to test with any rigor even macroeconomic models. There is no controversy about the reasons for this unhappy state of affairs, reasons that I have stated above. In few cases of interest do econometric techniques enable us to specify reliably the structural equations of the systems we are studying. If we are to arrive at such specifications, we must find additional sources of data, data that can give us realistic "priors".

Civil engineers do not rely simply on the laws of mechanics to design bridges, for those laws provide none of the parameters that describe the materials they are using. Nor do they estimate these parameters by applying simultaneous equations methods to existing complex physical structures. Instead, they retreat to the laboratory and measure directly the tensile and compressive strengths of the steel and concrete and other materials they intend to use. Meteorologists face even more difficult problems, since knowledge of the laws of the atmosphere is seriously incomplete, and is not derivable to the needed degree of accuracy from basic physical principles. To build models (e.g., for the purpose of predicting global warming), they must conduct extensive laboratory experiments on systems that are not wholly simple but that are far less complex than the Earth's atmosphere. Even then, their modeling is seriously handicapped by the coarseness of the global network of hourly and daily meteorological observations.

In neither of these cases of the physical sciences, parallel in many ways to the situation that faces macroeconomics, is sophistication in estimation of aggregated and noisy equations seen as the answer to the problems of accurate prediction. A large part of the scientific effort goes (wisely, I think) into laboratory study of component mechanisms and more precise direct measurement of initial and boundary conditions. We have hardly begun to exploit similar opportunities for obtaining better data in economics.

b. Laboratory Studies of Markets

An exceedingly promising source of data on the behavior of people trading in markets are the laboratory experiments on stylized markets that are increasingly being carried out by economists. After a long period during which data obtained from such experiments were regarded with great suspicion by journal editors and economists in general, they have now gained a certain level of respectability and acceptance. In fact, it has become positively stylish in leading economics departments to have at least one (but seldom more than one) faculty member engaged in experimentation. Vernon Smith, who was one of the pioneers in carrying out such experiments has recently published a collection of his empirical studies prefaced by a valuable brief history and assessment of these developments (V. Smith, 1991). I will not attempt here to summarize or evaluate experimental economics in detail, but will limit myself to a few general comments.

The early studies in this genre (beginning with Edward Chamberlin at Harvard) were designed as classroom demonstrations to show that markets "work" – i.e., stabilize at the equilibrium price. As the experiments were gradually elaborated, for example, to examine different market rules, new phenomena began to appear. Equilibrium was not always obtained rapidly and speculative "bubbles" were observed, sometimes quite spectacular ones.

When game theory was introduced to economists by von Neumann and Morgenstern (1944), it was at first investigated almost entirely with theoretical tools. The first important thing learned from the theory was that, in the context of a game between more than two players, or even in a two-person game that is not zero sum, it is exceedingly difficult to choose a definition of "solution", that is, a criterion of what constitutes rational play. Many definitions of rational play have been proposed, all of them producing peculiar results in some kinds of games. Failure to solve the problem of finding an incontestable definition of rationality gradually led game theorists to become curious about how human beings actually play games, and what notions of rationality seem to guide their behavior.

As game theorists began to take an interest in experimental economics, markets began to be studied where there were opportunities for collusion among the participants. Situations like the Prisoner's Dilemma produced phenomena that do not appear in simple competitive markets. For example, the strategy called "tit-for-tat" (cooperate with your opponent until he or she defects, then punish him or her on the next move), appeared frequently among human players, and showed a success that was hard to account for (except by hindsight) with a formal model.

This is exactly what a theory of bounded rationality leads us to expect. As long as decision situations are simple and transparent, people will be able to find and choose the alternatives that maximize their rewards. As soon as matters become more complex, the limits on their ability to discover the relevant information and to draw the right inferences from it will become more prominent in their behavior, and we will no longer be able to predict their choices on a priori grounds. To do so, we need theories of how they choose or construct the representations within which they view the game situation. These representations must incorporate strong assumptions about how the other players, also, view the game.

The difficulties will become especially acute in situations where the actors are trying to out-guess other actors. In any of these circumstances experiments become valuable tools for discovering what kinds of evidence people do, in fact, take into account, how they frame problems when they must simplify them to deal with them, and what methods they use to draw inferences and reach conclusions.

The early resistance to taking experiments on games and markets seriously as a source of data about how real markets operate was based partly on skepticism that students, offered small economic rewards for behaving "rationally", would have the same strength or direction of motivation as participants in real-world markets, where the stakes are generally much larger. As more and more economists have observed or carried out such experiments, I think this skepticism has largely faded.

There is much other evidence from experimental psychology that subjects will behave in experiments much as they do in the real world. Motivation must be provided for participation and for responding to profit goals, but there is much experience in psychology showing that if the inducements are sufficient to keep subjects' attention on a problem-like task, and they know how the game is "scored", they will address the task in a practical fashion and with strong motivation to perform well. Human beings are skilled role-takers – as evidenced by their frequent ardor for games in general, even including economic games like Monopoly. There is no reason why tasks of trading in an experimental market should fail to evoke motives and behaviors like those in real markets.

The rapid burgeoning of experimental economics is beginning to provide us with realistic theories of how markets work, theories that can also be tested with less systematic real-world observations and analyses of statistical aggregates. This research is beginning to provide us with some of the "priors" that we need to specify the structure of our econometric models of markets – the counterparts to the civil engineer's data on the strength of the steel used in a bridge.

Observation suggests that most empirical scientists use, in their research, the instruments and laboratory designs that they experienced during graduate and post-doctoral study. New instruments and new experimental paradigms do gradually appear, are taken up by the more able or venturesome, and, if useful, gradually diffuse through the discipline. The most important factor in speeding up this process is the rapidity with which the new instruments and paradigms are introduced as a part of the standard research training of graduate students.

One important reason why empirical economics of the past generation has consisted largely of econometrics, especially regression analysis, is that econometrics is the sharp weapon that graduate students have been trained to use. For reasons probably associated with the temporary hegemony of Positivism sometimes reinforced by "physics envy", these methods gained much higher status than historical studies, to say nothing of case studies of individual firms or individual decisions. Economists resemble other scientists in doing what they know how to do, and in reacting with deep skepticism to methodologies that do not fit their particular models of scientific method.

It is important, therefore, that adequate attention be given, by those using and advocating the methods of experimental economics, to developing further ways of testing the real-world validity of their experimental settings, and methods for drawing conclusions from experimental findings that can be used as prior information in the specification of models and in the interpretation of research using other methodologies.

c. Tests of the Postulates of Rationality

Somewhat different from laboratory studies of markets or of economic games are the experiments conducted by Kahneman and Tversky (1973), among others, seeking to determine by relatively direct means whether people make decisions that maximize expected subjective utility. The basic idea underlying the design of these experiments is to present people with several choices that will test whether the preferences revealed by them are consistent with each other. No assumptions are made in such a design about the respondents' utility functions other than that they should be consistent over several choices, as demanded by the theory.

In a well-known example of such an experiment, subjects are asked to suppose that they are suffering from a disease which will be cured by means of a risky surgical procedure if it is successful, but will certainly cause death within two years if the procedure is not performed. In one experimental condition, the subjects are told that there is a twenty per cent chance that they will die during surgery if they elect that option. In the other experimental condition, they are told that there is a eighty per cent chance that they will survive surgery and thereafter live a normal life. A substantially larger percentage of subjects elect surgery in the second condition than in the first, although the expected consequences, and their odds, are objectively the same in both conditions.

A large number of experiments of this kind show that, over a wide range of conditions, people do not make consistent judgments about uncertain events, violating the axioms of utility maximization and frequently violating the laws of probability. The situations in which they show such inconsistencies of choice and estimation are no more complex than the example cited above.

The Kahneman and Tversky experiments have been received by economists with a considerable degree of skepticism (just as was the early work in experimental economics that was described in the previous section), although interest in them, and willingness to publish the findings in standard economics journals has been slowly increasing. The main source of skepticism lies in whether people will behave in the same way in these question-and-answer situations as they would if confronted with the actual choice situation in real life. This is a fair question, although no explanations have been provided as to why the biases and inconsistencies exhibited by subjects should take the particular forms that they do.

What is striking about these experiments on choice under uncertainty is that they go to the very heart of the axiomatic structure of utility theory, throwing strong doubt on the veridicality of the theory as a positive description of human behavior. One would be hard-pressed to point to experiments in the natural sciences having such direct bearing upon basic theory that have been so casually treated. In those sciences, we can find frequent cases where theories had to wait a long time before being accepted, but few if any cases where data were simply ignored because they challenged the foundations of existing theory. No one ignored the data on black-body radiation that refuted the previous interpretations of these phenomena by Wien and (initially) Planck. No one challenged the facts of the photoelectric effect. The negative results of the Michelson–Morley experiment on ether drift were accepted as soon as the experiment was performed with sufficient accuracy to give a clear decision.

d. Laboratory Study of Problem Solving

Experimental markets comprise only one of the laboratory settings that can contribute to our knowledge of economic decision making. About thirty years ago there occurred in psychology a "cognitive revolution", which resuscitated older methodologies – rejected by Behaviorism – for studying complex human thinking, problem solving and decision making; and which introduced powerful new methodologies. The use of data from the verbal protocols of subjects who were thinking aloud while performing problem solving tasks acquired a sound methodological

79

foundation; and computers were introduced to simulate thinking processes, providing both a formalism for theory and an instrument for testing theory by simulating behavior.

Initially, verbal protocol data were viewed with suspicion by experimental psychologists, because of unsatisfactory experiences at the turn of the century with the method of introspection as a source of data. Careful testing, based on a review of the experimental literature on verbal reports of human subjects, together with new studies, gradually distinguished thinking-aloud protocols from introspective reports, defined the circumstances under which subjects would provide reliable reports, and developed valid procedures for using these reports as data (Ericsson and Simon, 1984, 1993). As a result, verbal protocols are now an important source of data in experimental psychology and in the engineering of expert systems.

Likewise, it took some years before cognitive psychology was comfortable with computer programs as theories of human thought processes. Psychologists had to come to understand that computer programs are systems of difference equations, having the same logical status as systems of differential equations in the natural sciences. Their new, and fundamentally important, property was that they enabled theories to be expressed in a variety of symbolic forms (e.g., forms that encompass natural language) without requiring the observables and the theoretical terms to be translated into the language of real or complex arithmetic. Acceptance of computer modeling was gradually gained by demonstrations of the success of such programs in simulating, step by step, the processes used by human subjects to solve difficult problems.

Verbal protocols and computer simulation of thinking, used separately or in combination, have produced an extensive and well-tested theory of human cognitive performance over a wide range of tasks, both laboratory tasks (e.g., playing chess or solving puzzles) and professional-level real-world tasks (e.g., making medical diagnoses, planning sequences of scientific experiments, diagnosing business problems from financial data, making investments in stocks and bonds).

Again, this is not the place to review the findings of this large body of research. Some summary of it can be found in Chapters 3 and 4 of the second edition of my *The Sciences of the Artificial* (Italian translation, *Le Scienze dell'Artificiale*, Il Mulino, 1988) or in John R. Anderson's textbook, *Cognitive Psychology* (1992). The theories that have been developed and tested successfully with the use of thinking-aloud protocols and computer simulation are theories of bounded rationality. They provide little evidence that utility maximization plays any significant role in human behavior over the range of situations that have been examined, or that optimization models permit behavior to be predicted, outside situations that subjects find simple and transparent.

To understand decision making, economic or other, it is not enough to see how choices are made from given sets of alternatives. We must also understand how problems arise and are framed, and how potential alternatives are generated. Fixing the agenda and settling upon problem representations and design procedures generally are far more consequential for outcomes than the final steps of choosing among given alternatives.

Again, the stage has been set, and early models provided, for expanding the application of these techniques to situations of interest to economics. To mention just two examples, models, based on bounded rationality assumptions, have been built of experts choosing stocks and bonds for trust portfolios (Clarkson, 1963), and of experts identifying company problems by examining financial statements (Bouwman, 1980). The speed with which these methods will diffuse within economics will depend on what steps are taken to make them known to economists, and on acceptance of studies using them as appropriate significant contributions to our economic knowledge.

5. Decision Making in the Business Firm: Case Studies

None of the methods of empirical research that I have discussed so far involve direct observation of behavior inside the business firm. Yet that is the place where the great majority of economic decisions are made. Several reasons can be given for the relative neglect of the business firm as a site for research. An obvious reason is the difficulty, real or imagined, of obtaining access. Another set of reasons have to do with designing a methodology that can obtain veridical data about actual business behavior. It is often asked whether businessmen can give an accurate account of their motives, or how they would behave under various circumstances.

The best answer to questions of getting access to business environments is to point to the substantial volume of research that has been based upon such access. I will mention just a few examples of which I have direct knowledge. In the 1950s, the faculty of the Graduate School of Industrial Administration at Carnegie Mellon University (then Carnegie Tech) engaged in extensive studies of decision making in business. A substantial study was made of the use (or non-use) of accounting data by sales and production managers in making their decisions, in four large companies (Simon *et al.*, 1954). Another was the series of studies directed by Richard Cyert and James March that were later incorporated in their book, *The Behavioral Theory of the Firm* (1963). As a third example, Holt, Modigliani, Muth and I (1960) developed a normative theory of production and employment smoothing in a firm, using data obtained from a paint manufacturer. Similarly, Abraham Charnes and William Cooper (1952) brought the new management science tool of linear programming to a large number of applied situations in industry.

All of these studies, descriptive and normative, took on, more or less, the character of case studies. That is, the task was to obtain a detailed view of behavior in a specific kind of situation, usually involving a sample of only one or a few firms. This was no great innovation, for one can assemble an enormous bibliography of case studies, carried out in most of the industrial countries of Western Europe as well as in the United States. Many of these were doctoral dissertations. In contrast with the studies mentioned in the previous section, in these kinds of studies it is not generally possible to obtain anything as detailed as thinking-aloud protocols of the actual thought processes. Nevertheless extensive empirical data can be obtained that track the decision process closely and that reveal both what data and what methods of analysis were used. Again, I will mention a single example.

Philip Bromiley (1986) gained access to four large American

firms in order to study how they made decisions about new capital investments – the volume of investment and the selection of particular projects. His methodology shows how one can obtain veridical information about such matters. He did not ask, "How do you go about making investments?" He requested and obtained access to data on the actual investments the firms had made in recent years, including rather specific data about individual projects and more general data about total rates of investment in new plant. He discussed with executives the organization structure and the processes that were followed in making these specific decisions, to determine what persons were involved; and, by interviewing these persons and examining their files, he found out what information was available and used (or not used) in making the decisions and what analyses were carried out. He produced a clear and detailed picture of the process in each firm which can be compared with the one postulated in one or another economic theory.

The procedures that Bromiley followed were based on extensive evidence from psychology that people can report accurately the processes they used in making specific decisions, especially if they are permitted to examine the written record while they make their responses. The evidence indicates that they are much less accurate when they are asked in general how they make decisions about certain matters. What safeguard is there against deliberately misleading answers? First, the studies are carried out under guarantees of personal and company anonymity that greatly reduce any motivation to deceive. Second, there are available the usual tests of consistency, where information is gathered from a number of different participants in the same events.

Another objection is sometimes raised to using case studies as a basis for theorizing about economic mechanisms: How can we generalize from behavior observed in one firm (or a small and not particularly random sample of firms) to an entire industry, or even economy? The short answer to this question is that a sample of one is better than a sample of none. The more complete answer is that only by beginning to look at firms, however small the initial sample, do we gradually obtain knowledge of how similar or divergent they are in their decision-making processes; about how many we need to sample in order to draw valid general conclusions; and what precautions we need to take to avoid bias in our samples.

I should not suggest that we are starting from scratch in these matters. In addition to the numerous research studies that have been carried out in firms, there have been even more studies, quite similar, aimed at providing case materials for teaching business subjects. The Harvard Business School, for example, has been collecting, for a half century, large numbers of cases on a whole range of business subjects, including production, finance, marketing, and business strategy. From the experience thus gained, a vast amount of knowledge and wisdom has been acquired about how to deal with the problems of subjectivity and selectivity in reporting, and of representativeness.

I address these points because, while case studies are quite familiar to many business school faculties, they are not to most faculties in economics departments. The wide experience of psychologists with the study of decision making by direct methods has not generally been shared by economists. As in the case of laboratory research, if economics is ever to make use of these new powerful, and even essential, methods, more and more economists must be brought into contact with them until they form a part of the normal training of economics doctoral students. This boot-strapping process is most likely to get its start in business school environments.

6. Economic History

Economic history should be a rich source of empirical data for economics, and of course it has been. Historical material provided Adam Smith with a major part of the empirical support for his theories. History that looks in detail at economic decision-making is a much more modern product; and, except for "biographies" of individual companies, often prepared in the context of studies of technological change, the study of organization and decision making processes within companies is a very recent entry into economic history, to which Alfred Chandler (1962) has made especially valuable contributions.

The problems raised by the use of historical materials for developing and testing economic theories are much like those raised by the use of case studies, but history has, in addition, all of the problems that econometricians encounter in the analysis of time series. Since economic history does have a niche, although a rather small one, in economics departments, it is perhaps somewhat less difficult than in the cases discussed previously to maintain a supply of economists who are adequately trained in using historical materials for these purposes. Beyond that, I have nothing to add on the subject.

7. Data from "Applied" Economics

The term "applied" is used in a rather curious way in economics, or at least in a way that is quite different from the usage in other disciplines. Every academic discipline is divided into a number of subdisciples. Even a field that places as high a value on general theories as physics does has a pattern of subfields: mechanics, electricity and magnetism, particle physics, the physics of continuous matter, and so on. Although problems in these fields are usually solved by *application* of general theories of mechanics, electromagnetism, quantum mechanics, statistical mechanics or thermodynamics, they are not regarded as fields of *applied* physics. They are simply parts of physics.

Theoretical physicists pay close attention to the experimental work in these fields, and new phenomena that appear in the laboratory are often the basis for substantial revisions of theory. Perhaps it is worth explaining why this is so. The fundamental theoretical structures of particle physics, relativity, and quantum mechanics can seldom be applied to complex atomic nuclei or structures composed of complex heterogeneous solid materials without extensive simplification and approximation. Therefore, microtheories grow up to explain these complex phenomena that are only loosely linked with the fundamental general theories. This is the case at present, for example, with respect to superconductivity.

In economics matters are treated differently. There is a domain of "theory" – principally microtheory, based on the unrealistic assumptions of global rationality, and a macrotheory that may be more or less closely linked to the microtheory. Everything outside this domain is referred to as "applied economics": labor economics, agricultural economics, industrial organization, the economics of the arts, and so on. But the latter are the fields in which economic decisions are made in the real worlds of government and business; and empirical observation in economics means observation of behavior that relates to one or more of these topics.

Words may be used as we like, but choices of usage are not without consequences. The consequence of applying the label of "applied" to all of the areas of economics where special phenomena occur has been to build a one-way conduit from "economic theory" to applied economics. Theory is something to be built by theorists, and then transported to applied economists, who use it to describe and interpret phenomena in their domain – not to test and revise the theory. A study of citations in economics will show that there is very little trickle-back from "applied" domains to theory. Theorists are not generally expected to be familiar in detail with the empirical data in the applied journals or to use them to test "theory".

In the other direction, it is conceived to be the job of "applied" economists to show how the events they study can be "explained" by the application of the received theory. In the language of the historian of science, Thomas Kuhn (1962), they are engaged in "normal" science, and are not expected to do "revolutionary", theory-altering science. Revolutionary economics lies in the province of the economic theorists. This attitude is deeply engrained in the profession. As an example, I quote from Douglass C. North's article on "Economic History" in the *International Encyclopedia of the Social Sciences* (vol. 6, p. 472).

There is no reason, of course, why the economic historian should be limited to received theory in economics. He is free to develop and apply theory of his own. However, caution in such an endeavor is obviously essential. The likelihood that the economic historian who is untrained in the principles of economics can derive theoretical propositions of any significance is very slim indeed. There is as wide a gap between common-sense observations in economics and economic generalizations as there is between common-sense observations in the physical sciences and the general laws of those physical sciences. We would not expect a layman to be able to derive from simple observations of physical properties the general laws of physics; nor can observations of economic phenomena lead an untrained economic historian to develop valid generalizations with respect to economic theory . . . The economic historian trained in economic theory will be well aware of the pitfalls inherent in economic analysis. Therefore, if he wishes to develop his own theoretical framework, he will take careful account of the work that has gone on before and the degree to which previous generalizations are supported by available evidence.

This statement contains some qualifications: the "untrained economic historian" is carefully distinguished from the "economic historian trained in economic theory"; the possibility of new theory emerging is not totally excluded. But the message is clear: mostly, the applied economist (in this case, the historian) takes theory obtained from the legitimated theorists and demonstrates that it explains the data he or she has observed. There is no corresponding warning to theorists that their theories must explain the phenomena unearthed by historians.

It would be both interesting and useful to have a study of the communication between economic theorists and economists in the areas of "application" to see whether the statement quoted above is characteristic of the actual relation between theoretical and applied economics. Lacking such a study, let me speculate a bit farther. In the physical sciences, "applied physics" is essentially engineering. This is *normal science* in the sense of Kuhn (1962), which operates within the framework of existing theory, perhaps even elaborates it, but does not seek to determine when it needs fundamental revision. "Revolutionary science", which challenges and modifies fundamental theory, takes place in physics rather than engineering, but, as we have seen, "physics" includes the principal domains of physical phenomena, it is not just "pure" theory without extensive empirical foundations.

The terminology in economics is either a cause of or a consequence of the tremendous reliance in the discipline upon deductive reasoning from premises that are regarded as being almost beyond challenge, and its rather imperious attitude towards data

– an attitude that assumes they are to be explained in terms of these unchallengeable assumptions.

8. Survey Techniques

Finally, I should like to mention some techniques for gathering empirical data, often called "survey methods", that have already had some application in economics but that deserve considerably wider use than they have had. They are not experimental in structure: that is, they do not try to manipulate the values of independent variables and to measure the consequent changes in the values of dependent variables. Instead, they are aimed at measurement of important parameters that appear in economic models. Instead of using econometric studies to measure them, they seek to determine them by direct questioning of economic actors.

George Katona (1951), and, following him, the Institute for Social Science Research at the University of Michigan pioneered this approach to estimating parameters. They were particularly focused on expectations and intentions: the estimates that economic actors themselves made about future events (changes in business conditions, the stock market, prices, and so on), and the economic actions they intended to take over the coming period (e.g., consumer purchases of captial goods, company capital investments).

The same kinds of doubts have been expressed about such studies as about the other "direct" procedures for learning about the economy that we have described. Can people provide reliable estimates of their own expectations, and of their intentions? Even if they can, will they? Experimental studies (Nisbett and Wilson, 1977) have cast substantial doubt on the ability of people to report accurately the motives for their actions. But I am not familiar with studies that throw any comparable doubt on their ability to report their expectations and intentions, and many studies (of both buying and voting behavior) show that intentions can be reported with reasonable accuracy, so that subsequent behavior is predicted correctly. It is expectations and intentions, rather than motives, that mainly concern us in estimating economic models.

Polling studies of expectations and intentions have been used in economic research to a considerable extent where the data have been available, but only modest progress has been made, since the polling techniques were introduced, to obtain such data with frequency, and on a large-scale basis for important economic variables. The sampling and aggregation problems that have to be faced in gathering and using such data are not severe.

9. Conclusion

Alternatives to neoclassical economics, including the theory of bounded rationality, have often been accused of attacking the existing theory without making concrete proposals for an alternative. In these essays I have tried to show that such a criticism is not warranted. First, the difficulties of the neoclassical theory are real, and ignoring them will not remove them. The theory is grossly inadequate for describing what goes on inside the business firm, for suggesting how economic decision making can be improved with the help of tools from operations research and management science, and for either understanding the events that occur in the whole economy or providing a basis for macroeconomic policy.

Nearly all of the conclusions reached by neoclassical theory that have the solidest empirical support (e.g., that demand curves slope negatively, supply curves positively, that excess demand drives prices up and excess supply drives them down) are reachable without the assumption that economic actors are maximizing or minimizing anything. Most of the conclusions that are drawn in the theory of public choice, or for application to various domains of "applied" economics do not rest on the assumptions of optimization, but do rest heavily on *ad hoc* assumptions about the content of the utility function (e.g., that people mainly want wealth, or power), and about the ability or inability of people to form accurate expectations (e.g., the money illusion).

Hence, most of the important conclusions of neoclassical economic analysis do not depend on the strict assumptions of neoclassical theory, but do depend strongly on matters of fact that are not settled by that theory, and can only be settled by observation. The alternatives to neoclassical theory do not depend any less on empirical facts. Their advantages are twofold: first, they embody much weaker assumptions about human rationality; assumptions whose validity has considerable empirical support. Yet they are able to reach most of the empirically validated conclusions reached by neoclassical theory on the basis of these weaker assumptions: dispensing with the need for a "principle of unreality", and meeting the test of Occam's Razor.

Second, a theory of bounded rationality focuses attention, as neoclassical theory does not, on the need for economics to strengthen and to greatly extend its procedures and practices for gathering empirical data. In this third chapter I have been concerned with describing the rich collection of procedures that is available to economics for finding out about the real world of economic behavior, and with pointing to the failures of contemporary economics to take advantage of the methods of research offered to it.

It is in the current generation and the coming generation of graduate students in economics that we must place our hope for the invigoration of empirical research in economics. In my contacts with academic departments of economics, both in the United States and in Europe, I find a high level of discontent, and even cynicism, with the existing state of affairs. Some students are fascinated by the mathematically sophisticated tools of mathematical economics, and acquire and employ them in complex intellectual exercises. Many more students view these mathematical tools with distrust and deplore the necessity of devoting their research time to formalisms that they regard as mainly sterile.

There is a joylessness in the profession at the need to "serve time" in order to be successful and prolific in publication, and ultimately to reach that state of "tenure" which crowns an academic career. Writing theory papers is seen as the route to a lengthy publication list, with a much larger output per hour than is obtainable from carrying out time-consuming experiments or field studies and analysing voluminous data.

The desire to explore new paths, including the path of empirical research – well beyond econometric studies – is there. But our students need our help if that desire is not to be frustrated. First, we need to revise the curriculum so that students of economics will be exposed to the range of empirical techniques that I have described, and will have opportunities to practice them while they are studying in the university. Second, we need to re-examine our procedures for judging manuscripts for publication, and our procedures for selecting and advancing faculty members so that the realism of theories will bear a larger weight in determining their interest and acceptability, and so that contributing to our factual knowledge about economic behavior and institutions will be appropriately evaluated and rewarded by the profession's decision processes.

If we move along these lines, we can look forward to new vigor in economics. The economic theories that are available today are sadly inadequate for dealing with the complex problems that our several countries and the world as a whole face. We cannot do less than strive to advance and improve those theories. Even modest progress in a discipline that is placed as strategically as economics is can have enormous value to the world of public and private affairs.

REFERENCES

ANDERSON J. R., *Cognitive psychology and its implications*, New York: W. H. Freeman, 1992, 3rd edition.

BECKER G. S., Irrational behavior and economic theory, *Journal of Political Economy*, 70, 1952, pp. 1-13.

BOUWMAN M. J., *The use of accounting information: Expert versus novice behavior*, unpublished doctoral dissertation, Pittsburgh PA: Carnegie Mellon University, 1980.

BROMILEY P., *Corporate capital investment: a behavioral approach*, Cambridge: Cambridge University Press, 1986.

CHANDLER A., *Strategy and structure*, Cambridge MA: Harvard University Press, 1962.

CHARNES A., W. R. COOPER and B. MELLON, Blending aviation gasolines, *Econometrica* 20, 1952, pp. 135-159.

CLARKSON G. P. E., A model of the trust investment process, in E. A. FEIGENBAUM and J. FELDMAN (Eds.), *Computers and thought*, New York NY: McGraw-Hill, 1963.

CYERT R. W. and J. G. MARCH, *A behavioral theory of the firm*, Englewood Cliffs NJ: Prentice-Hall, 1963.

DEARBORN D. C. and H. A. SIMON, Selective perception: the identifications of executives, *Sociometry* 21, 1958, pp. 140-144.

ERICSSON K. A. and H. A. SIMON, *Protocol analysis*, First and second editions, Cambridge MA, The MIT Press, 1984, 1993.

FRIEDMAN M., *Essays in positive economics*, Chicago IL: University of Chicago Press, 1953.

HOLT C. C., F. MODIGLIANI, J. F. MUTH and H. A. SIMON, *Planning production, inventories and work force*, Englewood Cliffs NJ: Prentice-Hall, 1960.

HOOD W. C. and T. C. KOOPMANS (Eds.), *Studies in econometric method*, New York NY: Wiley, 1953.

IJIRI Y. and H. A. SIMON, *Skew distributions and the sizes of business firms*, Amsterdam Neth.: North-Holland, 1977.

KAHNEMAN D. and A. TVERSKY, On the psychology of prediction, *Psychological Review* 80, 1973, pp. 237-251.

KATONA G., *Psychological analysis of economic behavior*, New York NY: McGraw-Hill, 1951.

KOOPMANS T. C. (Ed.), *Statistical inference in dynamic economic models*, New York NY: Wiley, 1950.

KUHN T. S., *The structure of scientific revolutions*, Chicago IL: University of Chicago Press, 1962.

VON NEUMANN J. and O. MORGENSTERN, *The theory of games and economic behavior*, Princeton NJ: Princeton University Press, 1944.

REFERENCES

NISBETT R. E. and T. D. WILSON, Telling more than we know: Verbal reports on mental processes, *Psychological Review*, 84, 1977, pp. 231-259.

NORTH D., Economic history, *International Encyclopedia of the Social Sciences*, v. 6., New York: Macmillan, 1968.

ROBERTS D. R., *Executive compensation*, Glencoe: The Free Press, 1959.

SIMON H. A., The compensation of executives, *Sociometry* 20, 1957, pp. 32-35.

SIMON H. A., *The sciences of the artificial*, 2nd edition, Cambridge MA: The MIT Press. (Italian translation, Bologna: Il Mulino, 1988).

SIMON H. A., G. KOZMETSKY, H. GUETZKOW and G. TYNDAL, *Centralization vs. decentralization in organizing the controller's department*, New York: The Controllership Foundation, 1954.

SMITH A., *The Wealth of Nations*, 5th edition. New York: The Modern Library, 1789 [1937].

SMITH V., *Papers in experimental economics*, Cambridge: Cambridge University Press, 1991.

DEBATE OF THE THIRD LECTURE

Interventions by Fabio Arcangeli, Anna Grandori, Andrea Ichino and Daniele Terlizzese.

QUESTION. Can you clarify the inference rules to be used in experiments and case studies?

SIMON. The question touches on one of the most important problems of methodology that faces us in using laboratory data, or for that matter, also case data from individual firms. Let me reflect a little on how that question is addressed in the field of psychology.

If you are just trying to find some generalizations about human behavior, then one of the things you can do is to run large numbers of experiments using college sophomores as subjects. Why college sophomores? Because there are lots of them accessible on a University campus. So if one were cynical one could say that the psychology one finds in the books on that subject is a psychology of college sophomores, and maybe that is not the same as the psychology of everyone else. Of course psychology does not stop there. It also studies the behavior of other people in comparable situations. There are some kinds of problems which have been used by psychologists for the study of problem solving processes, which have been used all the way up from five-year-old children to aged people. One thing you learn from such studies is that there are wide differences among people, and the study of individual differences has become itself a major topic within psychology. There are all sorts of techniques for characterizing individual differences.

Once you discover individual differences, the next thing you try to do is to reduce your variance by saying: can we find characteristics of the individuals that will predict their performance on this class of tasks and that will differentiate them? So we begin to build up a taxonomy much as biologists do: these kinds of people behave in this way, those kinds of people behave in that way. For example, in recent years there has been a significant number of studies (there need to be more) of differences between the behaviors of experts and novices in a task domain.

94

We give someone a brief description of Russia's agricultural problems and then ask that person: "You have to write a report for the minister. What should you say to him about these problems and how to deal with them?" Take as subjects some agronomists, some economists, some political scientists specializing in international affairs, some other political scientists specializing in Russian affairs, and see to what extent they think about the problem in the same way or in different ways.

From our theories of organizational identification we would expect to find characteristic differences. We would expect agronomists to talk about the problems of growing wheat in the Russian climate and soils; we would expect the political scientists to talk about the problems of organizing the Russian political system, and so they do. So already from the theories we have of organizational identifications with professional specialities we can begin to make predictions about the nature of those individual differences. There is no reason why we cannot build similar taxonomies with respect to business firms: the way that business executives with different responsibilities respond to situations.

The little experiment that Dewitt Dearbon and I ran, which I described in my Lecture, could be used in building such a taxonomy. In psychology we generalize from the individual by finding what different kinds of individuals there are. We thereby reduce the amount of variance in the behavior of individuals whom we have already characterized or in companies that we have already characterized as being this kind of company or that kind of company. Finding those variables, the critical variables that reduce the variance of our samples, is part of the science we are building and I think all of these ideas from so-called individual differences in psychology can be applied to our research in economics.

QUESTION. Why do you criticize so harshly econometrics? Econometrics was very useful in finding important stylized facts in many areas in economics. I think that econometrics and the kind of empirical analysis you suggest are complementary. Can you comment on that?

SIMON.   My first comment is that if the harsh criticisms on both sides have led some people like yourself to the kind of intermediate position you describe, in which you want to use both kinds of data, each to support the other, then that harsh criticism has not been in vain. I certainly do not want to see econometrics methods disappear from the face of the earth. I have been a Fellow of the Econometrics Society since 1954, although I have to confess that I no longer can read the articles in the journal with any great ease. I do not want to destroy econometrics. I want to be very realistic about what we can learn from econometric data, from other kinds of data and from the two used properly in combination with each other. I shall try to say a word about what I mean by "properly".

Of course, a sample size of a thousand is better than one if you can get the same data for the thousand that you can get for the one. That is not the usual choice. Usually it is a tradeoff between the kinds of superficial data that you typically can get in an econometric way and the deeper and more accurate data that you get in other ways. There is a real tradeoff as to the kinds of data you can get.

R-squares (measures of the per cent of total variance explained by the regression equations) are somewhat important; at least very low R-squares are signals of disaster, which tell you that you have not learned anything. R-squares do not avoid the identification problem. In order to understand why things happen and what will happen if we change them, it is not enough to have only reduced-form regressions. We have to have identified equations that reflect the causal mechanisms, and R-squares do not address that problem at all. To identify equations, we have to seek out additional facts from other sources. So I worry about that.

Yes, we have learned some stylized facts by econometric methods. I do not want to throw them away, but when I look at the journals today and the kinds of disputes that people have on macroeconomic policy, on monetary policy and the like, I find dozens of econometric studies that will show that rational expectations theory is just great and prove it from their equations, and I find other studies that find all sorts of things wrong with rational expectations and prove it with their equations. I do not think those disputes are going to be settled by econometric methods alone. Somehow, we have to deal with them in another way.

I referred earlier to the fact that the identification problem is intrinsic in the econometric method: you have $N \times M$ parameters and N equations, and you have to ask where are you going to get the other parameter values to identify your equations. Simply assuming that certain variables are uncorrelated in the real world does not do that, especially if you do not know factually that they actually are uncorrelated. All of the assumptions you make in order to get identifiability should be based on empirical evidence; they should not be simply a priori assumptions about what is or is not correlated with anything else.

It is precisely by using the other methods of inference that I am talking about that you can get additional evidence, allowing you to throw out certain equations as clearly not structural equations and to agree that different equations are the structural ones. Therefore, we should be using this other evidence as a major part of our econometric procedures, namely to guide the decisions we make in the course of defining the structure that we are going to estimate. Finally I think we should be careful about using that phrase, "qualitative evidence". When I write a computer program that simulates a person making a decision or solving a problem and that program follows closely, ten seconds by ten seconds, the path of that person, I do not see nearly as much room for subjective judgment as you imply. I think we simply have to find ways to objectify our data analysis in detailed decision studies just as econometrics objectified the methods we use in handling statistical data. By that very objectification we learned the limits of econometrics.

There are many ways of dealing with so-called qualitative data. There are all sorts of ways of asking people questions in a firm and some of those ways demonstrably lead to more objective data than other ways do. These ways need to be studied, they need to be improved and most of all they need to be transmitted to the next generation of economists through graduate training. So I do not think we have a quarrel, I think we have a job ahead of us: that is, a job of strengthening all of these methods so that we can tackle the difficult problems that we are concerned with.

QUESTION. Your opinion regarding the use of psychology in economics is not clear to me. Do we only have to learn about the methodology used in experimental psychology, or does psychology also have substantive results which can be useful to economics, for instance about the decision-making processes, the creation and selection of a set of alternatives and about how these alternatives are perceived?

SIMON. Yes, there is both a methodology in psychology today and there is a sizeable body of relevant substantive results about the decision-making process. Of course, there has to be division of labour in academia as elsewhere, but I do not think economists would find it too much of a burden to acquaint themselves with the main lines of the results of psychological research after a little sampling to decide how much of it might be relevant. Let me sell my own wares for a moment. A little book I published a few years age called *The Sciences of the Artificial*, which is available in Italian in the second edition (*Le Scienze dell'Artificiale*, Il Mulino, 1988), attempts to sketch out what some of the main results of modern cognitive research are without much application to economics specifically; but I think it would give some of the picture. So I do think that attention to the empirical results as well as to the methodology would be wise.

QUESTION. I wonder whether, in the theory of problem solving that you just announced, the discovery of new alternatives is an important part or not. More generally could you give us just a few hints on how you would go about building the theory of discovery of alternatives?

SIMON. The answer to the first question is yes, the theory does address discovering alternatives as well as testing them. In our laboratory in the last 15 years we have been addressing that question by building an empirically tested theory of scientific discovery. A book describing a large body of that work called *Scientific discovery* was published by the MIT Press. The authors are Langley, Simon, Bradshaw and Zykow. We took very important scientific discoveries as the phenomena to be explained. The reason we did this was that much of the previous research on creativity has used trivial tasks in the laboratory, so that after you have done research with such tasks nobody will agree that real creativity was studied.

If we take as our task discovering Kepler's third law from the same data that Kepler used, while there might be many objections to the research, one objection was ruled out: the objection that the discovery was not creative. Everyone agrees that Kepler was creative when he did that. So we took a large number of historical examples of scientific creativity, where we could give the computer exactly the same knowledge that the scientist had at that time and see whether we could create a set of processes that would make all of these discoveries. If we give Kepler's data to the computer program called BACON (named after Sir Francis Bacon), it will find Kepler's third law; if you give it the data that Joseph Black had when he mixed liquids together at different temperatures and found the equilibrium temperature, it will find Black's law; it will find many of the laws of the chemist, Dalton, and so on. We have tested BACON on a dozen or more examples.

In the course of doing that, BACON will sometimes discover that the data given to it and the concepts in which those data are expressed, acceleration or temperature or the like, are not all of the concepts it needs to state the law. In that case it has certain capabilities for inventing new concepts. For instance, given certain data about the mutual accelerations of bodies, it will invent the concept of inertial mass in order to explain those data. Given Joseph Black's data on temperatures of liquids, it invents, or reinvents I should say, the concept of specific heat. Today there are a number of research groups working on scientific discovery. There is also a substantial body of work (using thinking-aloud protocols more than computer simulations) on architectural and engineering design where the meat of the task is to find alternatives (designs). So, yes, there is a considerable body of work.

COMMENTS

CLAUDIO DEMATTÉ*

Herbert Simon's work is so vast and thorough – as the three lectures that we had the pleasure to listen to showed – that the discussant is forced to choose the subject of his/her remarks under the condition of bounded rationality. It is impossible, in fact, to foresee how the several branches of research pioneered by Simon will develop. Placed in front of such a rich choice of alternatives, all equally fascinating, I have trouble in properly drafting a ranking. Because of my background, however, I will direct my remarks to the nature of the firm, the point of departure and the heart of Simon's scientific contribution, as well as of the three lectures he presented.

Few scholars, maybe none, can be praised for being an extraordinary scholar of so many contiguous disciplines, as is Herbert Simon. His work provides a link, not only among the various branches of economics, but also between economics and other social disciplines.

Herbert Simon dedicated his professional life to the project of rebuilding economic theory, starting from the analysis of the decision-making unit of the economy and from observing their behavior. Unlike the neoclassical economists of the firm, Simon's construction begins with an observation that, in today's world, the economy is made up, for the most part, of organized decision-making units rather than of individuals operating in isolation. As he says in his second lecture: "It occurred to me also that any creature floating down to our earth from Mars would perceive the developed regions to be covered mostly by firms, these firms connected by a network of communications and transactions that we know as markets. But the firms would be more saliend than the markets, sometimes growing, sometimes shrinking, sometimes dividing or even swallowing one another. Surely they would appear to be active elements in the scene" (Second Lecture, p. 35).

This quote reveals why economists who study the firm love Herbert Simon's work so much. First of all, they share his starting point. The school of business and managerial economics that

* Università Commerciale Luigi Bocconi, Milano.

developed in Italy, at Bocconi University in particular, following the path breaking contribution of Gino Zappa, has always focused on the study of how firms are created, how they develop, why they become ill, and of why they often die, as we unfortunately observe too often in these times.

Because of this common approach, there are some noteworthy points of convergence between the work of Simon and the contribution of the Italian school of managerial economics. One of the most relevant aspects they share is the interest in the fundamental question of why firms come into existence. This problem is now almost obsessive in economic research. For a long period however, neoclassical economists just considered the firm as a simple production function.

Economists studying the firm used to consider the problem of why the firm sprang forth irrelevant. What purpose does asking why firms came into existence serve? The real problem should be to understand the laws explaining firms' dynamics.

The most attentive scholars, however, came to realize that an inquiry into the reasons for which firms sprang forth would have allowed them a better understanding of the essence of many problems of the economy of the firm: the crucial choices of "make or buy", the decision to diversify, the alternative between development through internal growth rather than through external agreements, etc.

In economic literature, we can now find several studies investigating why the firm ever appeared as an organized unit, composed of more persons, and why did it replace, for the most part, individual producers. Forerunners in defining or advancing this problem were Knight (1921), Coase (1937), and Alchian and Allen (1964). More recently, the contributions have greatly increased as new approaches to economic studies have developed: transaction cost economics, agency theory, the New Institutional Economics.

In his second lecture, Herbert Simon translates the question of why firms exist into a rather operative form. He asks why men give up individual production, opting instead to adhere to a "lasting project" of collective production. For Simon, the pursuit of the division of labor (that existed even at the time of

Adam Smith when the economy was populated by individual producers) is not the correct answer. Rather – he observes – it is the fact that the organization of the chain of production among individual producers often requires more complicated and long-lasting relationships than those deriving from simply fixing and paying a price for a good or service for its immediate delivery.

The more intense is the co-operation needed between the contracting parties, the more appropriate becomes a collective production process under the same organization versus a system of individual producers. However, the private entrepreneur who decides to become an employee must identify himself/herself with the collective project in order to minimize the costs of enforcing the labor contract.

Simon thus comes to define two of the fundamental conditions that determine the birth of the firm and its role: "The need for coordination, along with the possibility of creating organizational loyalties are perhaps two of the most important factors that give organizations an advantage over markets in many situations, and that account for the large role of organizations in the economic activity of a society like ours" (Second Lecture, p. 49). Like all great ideas, this problem might seem simple, even trivial. But let's reflect for a moment on the meaning of the two cornerstones on which, for Simon, the success of the firm is based.

On the one hand, he recognizes an objective element, different from activity to activity: "the need for coordination". When strongest, this need pushes towards organized production, while, when it is weakest, it leaves room for individual production, integrated by market transactions.

On the other hand, for Simon, the possibility of having collective production in a unified entity also depends on a factor common to all activity: the capacity "of creating organizational loyalties".

I will not go into length on the great implications of this contribution by Simon. It is enough to think of how it helps in understanding the industrial districts, true and proper organizational amoebae; in understanding the strength of the Japanese firms (in Japan, the capacity to create organizational identification is the highest); finally, in interpreting the lack of large firms in our country (in Italy, there are many difficulties in enforcing labor contracts, and both the ability and the possibility of creating firm loyalty seem smaller).

It is difficult to dissent from Simon's thoughts on the conditions which assure the superiority of the firm's organization with respect to the market. It seems to me, though, that the other conditions must be added to the two highlighted by Simon. Three more conditions seem important to me.

The first is connected with production technology. When production technology characterized by the presence of more workers is more productive than that available to individual producers, a trade-off appears for the individual producers: to continue as independent workers or become employees of a firm and participate in the larger value added of the collective production process. The choice will be a function of individual preferences and of the share of the greater value added produced by the collective production process which will be distributed to the employees.

A second reason that could propel workers to switch from independent to dependent employment – causing the firm to arise – lies in the possibility of choosing to become either employee or capitalist-entrepreneur. The latter offers capital and possibly organizational liabilities without prior pay negotiation for the contribution of his/her factors of production. Thanks to the positioning of the shareholders-entrepreneurs, rewarded with the residual gain from the production process, the income uncertainty for dependent workers is reduced. Agents with strong risk aversion would choose to be employees just because of the lower, but more certain, income.

There is a further element that can explain why firms have successfully replaced individual entrepreneurs. Simon – and I find myself in complete agreement – affirms that the main task of a firm is not to set prices and quantity, but to "design" the product, the marketing strategy, and the structure of the production process. The possibility of participating in a productive project of higher collective value added depends on the "organization" of labor around a superior entrepreneurship, a very scarce factor of production.

If we add the three conditions indicated above to the two of Simon's we can better describe why we have passed from an economy populated by individual producers to one where firms prevail. Simon's logical scheme then becomes a powerful instrument for investigation and forecasting.

Another aspect of Simon's work deserves attention: how can the assumption of individual behavior based on the maximization of one's own welfare be compatible with the existence of the firm that, instead, assumes employees will behave so as to maximize the firm's profits? There are two aspects to this thorny question that must be kept distinct. The first consists of choosing the behavioral assumptions that explain the actions of both individuals and organizations. The second is related to the question of how it is possible to reconcile the individual's objectives with those of the organization.

Regarding the first point, all of Simon's work aims at confirming how human behavior is geared to the logic of "satisfying", rather than to that of maximizing. Given the conditions under which the choices are made, man can only be bounded rational. This is particularly true regarding the choice that absorbs the major part of the work directed at managing the firm and that determines the survival itself of the firm: the choice of the "design" (the term used by Simon) of products, of the production process, of the marketing policy in combination with the choice of a complete business strategy. In this case, the crucial aspect of the decision process is not the choice in and of itself, but the "identification problem". In fact, it is much more difficult to elaborate the alternatives than to choose among them, since there are many possible alternatives. Their identification and estimation of the related costs-benefits are costly operations subject to enormous uncertainty. In brief, nothing is as important for the firm as the choice of its strategy. For this choice, however, bounded rationality conditions are even stronger than for any other decision.

In short, the assumption that choices are taken under conditions of bounded rationality is the inevitable starting point of any studies on managerial economics.

I now turn to the problem of the reconcilability of individual objectives with the life of the firm. Simon points out that for the neoclassical economists, an apparent insoluble problem exists: if the employees follow – as the theory assumes – their objective of personal utility maximization, how can the firm survive? Its survival would, in fact, need everyone participating in sharing the common profit objective.

Simon criticizes the school of the New Institutional Economists for its propensity to identify the mass planning of contracts as the central issue, respectful of the incentive compatibilty constraints.

Simon dismantles this line of reasoning by revealing two simple facts:

1. there is evidence that, in the real world, this pressing need for enforcement does not exist;

2. the impossibility of conciliating employee and firm objectives.

For Simon, the compatibility between self-interested employee behavior and the common profit goal comes about as a result of an "organizational identification", which is in turn a form of altruism, a natural product of the neo-Darwinist gift to "human docility" and of bounded rationality.

The construction is fascinating, but can be perfected. For this purpose, I will use one of the principles Simon proposes in his third lecture: the principle of parsimony suggests using weak rather than strong assumptions in the construction of theoretical models. I thus pose this question: Do we really have to assume altruism to reconcile the otherwise divergent objectives of individual employees and of the firm? In other words, is it really necessary to the development and survival of the firm that all the participants of a long lasting collective project between suppliers of capital and workforce behave altruistically, in the sense defined by Simon? Can we substitute this strong assumption with a weaker one? I think so, and, in so doing, we might even be able to better explain the nature of the collective decision-making process of organizations. Even though the agents participate in the collective project with selfish motives, coercion may be unnecessary for the pursuit of the objectives of the firm. In fact, when all agents in the firm realize that they would lose the benefit of their joint work if they did not respect the profit objective, they would find themselves facing a dilemma. They may play selfishly with the risk of seeing the collective project vanish or they may reject the opportunistic behavior that would maximize their own interests subject to their participation in the firm. Although this second solution is not an optimum, given their participation in the firm, it may probably be an improvement over the alternative that could be obtained outside the firm. If, as a result of collective short-sightedness, employees try to maximize their personal objectives, thereby cancelling the rewards of their residual claimers, those who hold the equity capital, the firm would cease to exist. And in fact, many do go bankrupt.

The theoretical framework that I propose allows for the possibility of opportunistic or short-sighted behavior on the part of employees. Moreover, it recognizes that whenever such behavior is not resisted, the collective project could crumble since the partners who come out damaged would not have any motive to continue supporting the project.

It is therefore necessary to use managerial experience to foster the natural tendency for understanding and accepting the collective game by the firm's participating agents as well as to prevent opportunistic behavior. Appropriate management of (their) positive and negative attitudes is, therefore, the critical factor for the firm's success.

In addition to its correlation with the Simonian argument of bounded rationality, this approach recognizes how the firm's choices derive from collective decision-making processes. As such, these choices are outcomes of different abilities, preferences, knowledge biases, and of the opposing forces of the various agents committed to the firm in different forms.

I would have liked to offer some remarks on the research methods and interdisciplinarity of Simon's work. Unfortunately, the pre-set time limits prevent me from doing so.

In closing, however, let me express my most hearty thanks and admiration to Professor Simon.

MASSIMO EGIDI*

1. The Choice Between Organizations and Markets

In "The Role of Organizations in an Economy" Herbert Simon focuses on a number of issues which are crucial for clarification of the relationships between economics and organizational theory. In particular he gives a new perspective on what has become a classical question of economic theory: can the firm and the market be regarded as two alternative forms of the organization of economic activity?

The entire question stems from Coase's celebrated article "The Nature of the Firm"[1] written in 1936, in which he compares firm and market and suggests that they are two economic institutions that perform the same task – the coordination of decisions taken by various individuals – in different ways. As in the market, so within the firm dispersed knowledge and different skills are coordinated. Within the firm, Coase notes, coordination takes place through orders and control, in markets through the price system.

In the following pages I will discuss some of the problems arising from Simon's lecture, which, in relation to the New Institutionalists' interpretation of the problem, offer us a very different and illuminating perspective on the relationship between market and organizations.

In his lecture, Simon observes that a key point in analyzing Coase's intuition is to decide what meaning is to be attributed to the term "coordination". We may therefore conveniently begin by examining what common aspects and what differences can be found between coordination by markets (which comes about through competition) and coordination "by managers" within a firm.

It is widely known that analysis of coordination by the market has developed in different versions within the neoclassical school: from Smith's "invisible hand" to Walrasian "tâtonnement", to

* Università degli Studi, Trento.
1. COASE R., "The Nature of the Firm" in *Economica*, n. 4, 1937, pp. 386-405.

von Hayek's "competition as a procedure for discovery of the new", to mention only some. This is not the place to review these various versions; nevertheless it should be pointed out that, despite their differences of emphasis, all schools agree over the fact that coordination is a process by which different plans decided independently by different individuals becomes mutually compatible.

A further feature is ascribed to the coordination process: namely that it is a learning procedure by means of which equilibrium prices are "discovered". This feature, which has been emphasized in particular by the Austrian school, is nevertheless also present in the Walrasian formulation. In Walras' analysis, in fact, coordination takes place through tâtonnement: the auctioneer receives all information concerning excess demand and issues all information concerning prices. The interaction between auctioneer and agent can be interpeted as a process of collective learning which enables economic agents to discover the equilibrium: that is, the parameter values by which their plans become mutually compatible. Interestingly, this type of learning cannot be assimilated to the process of individual rational choice; on the contrary, it is a multi-actor cooperative process in which the part played by each agent is extremely limited, and the final result is achieved without the individual agent being aware of it; that is, the agent does not engage in an individual search for equilibrium prices. This is the third essential feature of coordination.

We may therefore sum up the argument so far by saying that the coordination performed by competition has three important properties:

1. different plans of separate individuals, drawn up independently and rationally, become mutually compatible;

2. the economic system "discovers" the correct parameter values, i.e. the equilibrium prices, which enable coordination to take place;

3. The discovery process is one in which agents are unaware.

Hence, albeit in embryonic form, coordination is interpreted as a learning procedure realized through competition.

Let us now turn to the coordination that takes place within economic organizations. Is this process, as Coase suggests, analogous to coordination carried out by the invisible hand? Can we consider it to be a competitive process which coordinates the plans of separate individuals through a system of orders and thus induces individuals unwittingly to reach some kind of "internal organizational equilibrium"?

Let us inspect the differences between the two cases. For the first characteristic above to be respected (the mutual compatibility of plans), one must assume that agents within organizations – here employees and managers – take their decisions and formulate their plans entirely independently of one another, like the agents in a Walrasian atomistic economy. That they do not behave in this way is a well-established fact.

Thus the description of the coordination process provided by the Walrasian model cannot be realistically extended "inside the black box" without introducing substantial modifications into the most important features that Walras attributed to individual planning.

Instead of trying to define these modifications, as an alternative research strategy we should examine if there exists an organizational set up which provides individuals with all relevant information, as in the Walrasian picture of "tâtonnement".

A model of this kind must have the following features: first, the tasks of the individuals within the organization must be perfectly identified and rigidly separated, as in the tayloristic caricature of the organizational machine; second, individuals (employees and managers) must decide and realize their plans following a general plan issued by a central coordinator.

Only under these conditions can we avoid the unrealistic assumption that individuals are able to perform very complex calculations without costs, because all the computational effort is undertaken by the central coordinator.

This picture of planning, which transfers the Walrasian framework within the organization, was provided by Barone[1] at the beginning of the century, when he showed that the Minister of planning in a collectivist society can issue appropriate orders

1. BARONE E., "Il ministro della produzione nello stato collettivista". *Il Giornale degli Economisti*, agosto-settembre 1908.

and perfectly govern the economy on the basis of the same principles as the Walrasian general equilibrium model.

Agents in this case send information and receive orders via the central coordinator, which, in turn, receives information and sends orders. The main problem arising from this model is explaining how it is possible for the central coordinator to obtain and process all relevant information. In fact, whereas the Walrasian auctioneer issues "orders" simply by altering the prices on the basis of the aggregate excess demand, the tasks to be performed by the Minister of Planning are more complex: he must transmit the correct order to every producer. Consequently he must have detailed knowledge of the economic system and its evolution over the time. It was the Austrian School in the 1930s (von Wiese,[1] von Mises and von Hayek in particular) that first addressed this question and denied the possibility of central planning in a collectivist society. Even if we may not fully agree with this position, it is very difficult to admit that such a hyper-centralized system would be able to adapt to external changing circumstances: individuals in this context would mechanically execute the orders, without any autonomous capacity to decide or to plan. A business organization based on this kind of rigid and centralized planning would lack in endogenous mechanisms of reaction, and therefore would be unable to change and to survive in a competitive market.

In consequence, a key problem is to understand if, beyond the mechanism of centralized planning, it is possible to model different coordination mechanisms characterized by different degrees of decentralization; and what level of individual knowledge, information processing and planning capacity they require. To move in that direction we must make more realistic assumptions about the individual planning activity, and revise the traditional opinions on the independence and rationality of decisions.

As a first assumption, it is necessary to take into account that individual plans are formulated in a strategic context, i.e. that they depend on the plans implemented by other individuals;

---

1. WIESE, VON L., "Die Konkurrenz, vorwiegend in soziologisch-systematischer Betracthung" in Verhandlungen des 6. Deutschen Soziologentages, 1929.

therefore the higher the decentralization of the coordination mechanism the greater is the amount of computation required of individuals to evaluate all the consequences of their decisions.

Second, and more important, we must acknowledge that within organizations the separation of knowledge and skills among employees is not total; nor can it be among firms.

This viewpoint seems related to Simon's opinion, where he points out that "... neoclassical theory assumes that there are clear boundaries between the elements known as firms. In practice these boundaries are highly ambiguous ... Markets represent only a part, if an important part, of the channels of communication and coordination between organizations".

Indeed, the production of knowledge and information within a firm is not based on a rigid separation of skills and knowledge among economic agents, as happens in the Walrasian market. On the contrary, an organization is usually based on close interaction among its components, on the joint use of competences, and on the exploitation of the positive externalities which arise from interactions. Within organizations, individuals exchange information and orders, as Coase suggests, but they also exchange knowledge and alter their competences and skills.

This is a crucial difference from Walrasian assumptions, and suggest us to distinguish between "static" and "dynamic" planning.

The former takes place when individual planning does not involve any change in the organizational shape, as in Walras and Barone's accounts. (A more or less centralized coordinating mechanism can render different individual plans reciprocally compatible, by means of orders and information channels.)

The latter takes place when individual plans modify the organizational shape; coordination in this eventuality can be assimilated in to a (deliberate, conscious or unconscious) process of organizational design.

The two features I have emphasized – interdependency of individual plans and overlapping competences among individuals – suggest that, to find an explanation of the relationship between economic organizations and individual behaviours, we must move beyond the limits of the Walrasian approach.

2. Bounded Rationality, Coordination and Learning: from Hayek to Simon

Hayek went to the root of the problem of the relationship between individual rationality and the role of the market by incorporating it into the more general problem of the role of knowledge in society, and by examining the nature of economic institutions.

His point of departure was a critique of the manner in which the general equilibrium model had traditionally been interpreted. The model assumed the consumer preferences as "given" and all the technologies as freely available.

In his Presidential Address of 10 November 1936 at the London Economic Club, Hayek contested this aspect of the model. He pointed out that, although technologies and preferences are indeed the givens of the problem, they are unknown to the majority of economic agents: they constitute idiosyncratic, specific, personal information and knowledge whose acquisition by economic agents would require unlimited capacities of memory and calculation.

Under the (Walrasian) hypothesis that agents have consistent preference sets, know all available technologies, and possess an unlimited capacity for calculation and memorization, they may be able to make fully rational decisions. By removing these unrealistic assumptions, and emphasizing that knowledge is diffused heterogeneously and asymmetrically among individuals Hayek implicitly assumed that the rational and cognitive capacities of the individual are limited. He can be considered a precursor of Simon's bounded human rationality approach, because his major hidden premise to the explanation of why economic institutions exist is that individuals have limited capacities and competences.

In restating this point, Simon notes that it is precisely because individuals are incapable of handling all the relevant knowledge and information necessary for rational decision making that economic institutions exist. He maintains that knowledge is efficiently accumulated and transmitted by institutions, which fulfil tasks which are beyond the individual capacities. The role of the institutions is therefore paramount: they gather knowledge and information in such a way as to reduce the uncertainty of human action and broadly extend its range.

Note that it is not only realistic but logically consistent to assume that no single actor is able to possess a complete and accurate picture of all relevant information and knowledge; should such an actor exist, this would annul the necessity itself of the economic institutions (and particularly of the market). A lucid restatement of this point, as part of a critique of the theory of rational expectations, is to be found in Arrow.[1]

Hayek attributes a broader role to competition than was envisaged by the Walrasian model. In a number of celebrated passages he describes competition as a process of discovery of the new; a process whereby individuals obtain the specific information they need to formulate and implement their plans. The central point, in his view, is that the economic institutions reflect the way in which the division of labour and knowledge among the different individuals in society has come about, and they guarantee its coordination.

". . . I still believe that, by what is implicit in its reasoning, economics has come nearer than any other social science to an answer to that central question of all social sciences: How can the combinations of fragments of knowledge existing in different minds bring about results which, if they were to be brought about deliberately, would require a knowledge on the part of the directing mind which no single person can possess? To show that in this sense the spontaneous actions of individuals will, under conditions which we can define, bring about a distribution of resources which can be understood as if it were made according to a single plan, although nobody has planned it, seems to me an answer to the problems which has sometimes been metaphorically described as that of the 'social mind' ".[2]

According to Hayek, the market is a non-constituted institution. Like language and money, economic institutions are not born of a fully intentional and rational collective decision; nor

---

1. ARROW K. J., "The Future and the Present in Economic life" in *Economic Inquiry*, n. 16, 1978, pp. 157-170.

2. HAYEK, VON F. A., "Economics and Knowledge" in *Individualism and Economic Order* (Reprint of 1948 first printing) Chicago, The University of Chicago Press, 1980.

are they the outcome of a project generated by the mind of a social architect. They are – in his view – the historical and unintentional product of the consolidation of inter-individual relationships. However, Hayek does not address the problem of how institutions emerge, or how "spontaneous" institutions and artificial institutions, i. e. those created by conscious human design, can coexist and interact.

But do completely artificial institutions actually exist? And if they do, in what relation do they stand with "natural" ones? Hayek considered socialist planning to be the limiting case of artificial structures, in direct contrast to the natural mechanism of competition. Much of his work was devoted to demonstration of the impossibility of economic planning, or better to his contention that planning is not an institutional instrument able to replace the market effectively – the planner, unlike the market, is unable to gather all the information and knowledge required to reach an optimum solution.

But, as Coase remarked one year later on Hayek's Presidential Address, planning is the characteristic feature of any business organization, and therefore at least up to a certain point planning activity is expected to be efficient.

Organizations, the pioneering book written in 1958 by March and Simon, proposes a different and richer view, where hierarchical planning and designing – which typically are sciences of the artificial – and individual "spontaneous" decisions are interrelated.

Before developing this point, I conclude the discussion about the Walrasian framework by suggesting that the appropriate context to compare market and organization as alternative cooperation devices, is not the Walrasian one, but, more promisingly, the Hayekian one.

The reason for the failure of attempts to apply the Walrasian framework directly to what happens within organizations therefore seems now clear: the Walrasian model assumes a world in which the division of labour is given; there is a complete separation of skills and knowledge among economic agents, and the creation or transfer of knowledge and skills is assumed to be either impossible or costless. The previous discussion suggests that coordination requires a more complex explanation, which takes account of the capacity to innovate and learn of individuals and organizations, in a context related to limited rationality and knowledge sharing. Hayek, and later Schumpeter, assume a world in which the creation of knowledge is the fundamental process underlying coordination activities and more generally economic change. But they did not provide clear theoretical microfoundations on which to model economic change. With bounded rationality theory Simon give, us the first important step in that direction. It is therefore convenient to turn to the problem of knowledge acquisition and creation, along the lines of Simon's approach, to evaluate the potentialities of these assumptions in explaining the nature of cooperation within organizations.

3. Organizational Learning: Microeconomic Aspects.

The idea that the learning activity plays a central role in human decision making derives from the pioneering work of Cyert, Simon, March and Newell. In 1956, in a path-breaking article which constituted a first crucial step in analyzing rationality within organizations, Cyert, Simon and Trow carried out an empirical analysis of managerial decisions which revealed an evident "dualism" of behaviour:

"Decisions in organizations vary widely with respect to the extent to which the decision-making process is programmed. At one extreme we have repetitive, well defined problems (e. g., quality control or production lot-size problems) involving tangible considerations, to which the economic models that call for finding the best among a set of pre-established alternatives can be applied rather literally. In contrast to these highly programmed and usually rather detailed decisions are problems of non-repetitive sort, often involving basic long-range questions about the whole strategy of the firm or some part if it, arising initially in a highly unstructured form and requiring a great deal of the kinds of search processes listed above".[1]

1. CYERT R. M., SIMON H. A. and TROW D. B., "Observation of a Business Decision" in *Journal of Business*, n. 29, 1956, pp. 237-248; SIMON HERBERT A., *Models of Man*,

March and Simon[1] note that in conditions well-structured from the cognitive and decisional viewpoint, subjects learn to solve problems, achieve a stable behavioural pattern of actions or, if one wishes, their behaviour becomes routinized. The sequence of choices confronted by individuals performing an organizational task constitutes a repetitive procedure which becomes familiar to those executing it, and presents well-defined alternatives codified according to the variants arising from changing external circumstances.

Most of the human activity within economic organizations takes the form of this procedural and routinized behaviour. Within the organization, we can consider as routine any procedure which provides for the execution of a specific task; it is therefore a procedure which solves a set of problems internal to the organization. A procedure can be described as a set of instructions determining the actions to be taken when dealing with a particular circumstance.

It seems natural, therefore, to model a procedure as a program, in the specific sense given to the term by computation theory, as a list of instructions in an artificial language. This enables us to represent procedures formally and to model procedural rationality.[2]

If individuals are able automatically to replicate repeated sequences of decisions deriving from their interactions with others, the role of routines becomes clear: they enable individuals to save on "rational computation" and radically reduce the complexity of individual decisions. In consequence a part of everyday decisions becomes to some extent "automatic" and therefore possibly tacit. More precise exploration of this point has been conducted by Nelson and Winter,[3] on the basis of the methodological principles enunciated by M. Polanyi in *Personal Knowledge*.[4] They emphasize that some behavioural sequences consist of actions which are par-

New York, Wiley, 1957; CYERT R. M. and MARCH J. G., *A Behavioural Theory of the Firm*; SIMON and NEWELL A., *Human Problem Solving*, Englewood Cliff, Prentice Hall, 1972.

1. MARCH J. G. and SIMON H. A., *Organizations*, New York, John Wiley, 1958.

2. MARCH and SIMON, *cit.*, ch. 6.

3. NELSON R. R. and WINTER S., *An Evolutionary Theory of Economic Change*, Cambridge (Mass.), The Belknap Press of Harvard University Press, 1982.

4. POLANYI M., *Personal Knowledge: Towards a Post-Critical Philosophy*, London, Routledge and Kegan, 1958.

tially tacit; this feature leads the two authors to the problem of how tacit knowledge is formed, transferred and stored in memory.

This is a starting point for exploring how cognitive skills, which arise through experience and cooperation, are stored in the memory and by consequence become building blocks for subjects who have to solve problems. Pursuing this line of research, Cohen and Bacdayan[1] suggest that routines are stored as procedural memory. Following Squire's distinction between procedural and declarative memory, they claim that "procedural memory appears to be the form that stores the components of individual skilled actions – for both motor and cognitive skills. It is distinguished from declarative memory, which provides the storage of facts, propositions, and events".[2]

Cohen and Bacdayan use a laboratory experiment to analyse the emergence of procedural behaviour by two subjects involved in a game which requires coordination and cooperation, and its "sedimentation" in memory. The general point at issue here is how the acquisition, and memorization of cognitive skills takes place, and how its transfer is possible, i.e. how skills can be reused. As Singley and Anderson show,[3] the range of transfer of procedurally encoded skills is very restricted. By consequence, learning requires effort and time, and the transmission of cognitive skills is at least partially opaque.

Moreover, routines memorization is highly local and incomplete, and it therefore pre-supposes the human capacity to complete missing knowledge. This feature emerges both in theoretical[4] and empirical frameworks[5] (Singley and Anderson, 1989), (Cohen and Bacdayan, see note 3, p. 120).[6]

1. COHEN M. D. and BACDAYAN P., "Organizational Routines Are Stored as Procedural Memory: Evidence from a Laboratory Study", University of Michigan, mimeo, 1958.

2. SQUIRE L. R., *Memory and Brain*, New York, Oxford University Press, 1987, p. 5.

3. SINGLEY M. K. and Anderson J. R., *The Transfer of Cognitive Skill*, Cambridge (Mass), Harward University Press, 1989.

4. CHAITIN, *Algorithmic Information Theory*, Cambridge: Cambridge University Press, 1987.

5. SINGLEY M. K. and ANDERSON J. R., *The Transfer of Cognitive Skill*, Cambridge (Mass.), Harvard University Press, 1989.

6. EGIDI M., "Routines, hierarchies of problems, procedural behaviour: some evidence from experiments", IIASA Working Paper WP-94-58, forthcoming in K. ARROW *et al.* (editors), *Rationality in Economics*, MacMillan, 1993.

Individuals involved in games which require cooperation, after the initial period of learning, do not memorize the detailed steps of organizational procedures; they do not keep all knowledge and information they need to play stored in memory, but create and memorize sets of simple "meta rules" which allow to re-create the organizational routines. These rules are elementary "Condition-Action" rules (in the standard sense of the cognitive sciences), which are the result of sub-goals identification, i.e. of a spontaneous division of knowledge among agents. Agents store in procedural memory these rules, which embody mutual relations and enable them jointly to recreate the routines at any particular moment.

To summarize some of the previous issues: even if we are still far from being able to frame the complex problem of knowledge creation and transmission within a unique theoretical approach, the assumption that procedures are the micro-units of human behaviour in organizations is strongly confirmed by observations, field research and experiments. They are partially tacit, opaque and incomplete. The latter property is particularly relevant because of its consequences on organizational change: the fact that individuals do not usually possess full knowledge of organizational procedures, but are able to recreate its missing components, implies that they have the capacity to solve micro-problems autonomously. The problem is now to clarify the relationship between this kind of micro-innovative activity and top–down planning and designing managerial activity in order to better understand how organizational change take place.

4. Organizational Learning and the Division of Knowledge

When managerial decisions are taken in ill-defined and uncertain conditions, one successful strategy of solution is based on the attempt to decompose the problem to be solved in to sub-problems easier to approach. This procedure, carefully analysed in Organizations, is now becoming a classic approach to problem solving in Artificial Intelligence.[1]

1. NEWELL A., SHAW J. C and SIMON H. A., "Elements of a theory of human problem solving" *Psychological Review*, 65, 1958, pp. 151-66.

A well-known feature of this procedure is recursivity: subjects seek to decompose the problem to be solved into sub-problems which they hope will prove easier for them to handle. If some of these sub-problems are still too complex, they are in turn decomposed. The procedure continues recursively until easily solvable sub-problems have been obtained. If successful, the decomposition procedure structures the original problem into a hierarchy of inter-related sub-problems.

This procedure is typical of top–down planning activity within organizations; it gives rise to a recursive division of tasks which, if achieved successfully, can be used by the top management to give a new shape to the division of labour, knowledge and competences within an organization.

This does not mean that the hierarchized structures which perform different but inter-related tasks within organizations are the outcome of a purely artificial and centralized process of planning; on the contrary, planning and organizational design can be, to a certain extent, distributed activities.

It is now convenient to recall the distinction between planning (static planning) and organizational designing (dynamic planning). In the first case an organizational hierarchy is supposed to be "given" with a related division of labour and coordination mechanisms; individuals, at different hierarchical levels and with different competences, may have discretionary power in realizing a general plan (top–down planning), or they may actively propose new solutions, new "local" plans, which are coordinated by means of non-centralized mechanisms (for example, bottom–up planning). But they formulate their plans according to a given division of labour.

In the second case the activity is to design new organizational solutions: the problem is to change the organizational structure, i.e. the division of labour and the coordination mechanism.

Turning our attention to the first case, note that, even if they operate through strongly hierarchized structures, organizations in the real world do not require their operational units merely to

---

1. NEWELL A. and SIMON H. A., *Human Problem Solving*, Englewood Cliffs, NJ: Prentice-Hall, Inc., 1972.

execute procedures, or blindly to implement plans meticulously set out by the upper levels of the hierarchy; on the contrary, within real organizations people continuously modify procedures and adapt them to external change.

Therefore, even when planning is a top–down centralized activity, it has a "conjectural" character, for bounded rationality reasons: on the one hand, in fact, the higher levels of the hierarchy must formulate plans in extremely general and open-ended terms, because the ways to implement general plans into details are not and cannot be known a priori and computed; on the other, the lower levels do not merely execute perfectly defined and detailed plans in a "mechanical" fashion. Execution of plans requires the ability to interpret and to adapt general ideas, and to solve problems and conflicts that arise so that these ideas can be implemented.

I now turn to the case of organizational design. As in the previous case, consider a situation between the two extreme alternatives, respectively the centralized and the distributed coordination of designing activity. Suppose that the top management puts into place a re-design of the organization in order to react to some kind of environmental change. Again, the implementation of the new division of labour within the organization which is required by such a change gives rise to a complex process of adaptation which is far from that believed by the traditional theory of planning: from one hand in fact the implementation of a new organizational design requires managers and employees to re-think their jobs and revise their competences; from the other, to be effective, any new design requires local checks and readjustments, i.e. the resolution of cognitive conflicts arising from the match among the general requirements of the project and the specific, idiosyncratic knowledge arising from the personal knowledge of any single agent.

We can conclude that the micro-problem-solving activity is a fundamental source of organizational change, which displays its effects also beyond the scope of the individual activity within the organization. Individuals have very incomplete knowledge of the organizational routines, as we have seen, but they have the ability to recreate the missing parts of it: they can modify and adapt general plans to specific contexts or micro-innovate, i. e. find new local solutions to the problems, whatever their position in the hierarchical pyramid may be. When applied to organizations, the ability to complete knowledge suggests an explanation of how organizational procedures develop and change, because it allow us to attribute to individuals a permanent ability to micro innovate and to modify procedures.

A question implicitly arises from our discussion: why are realistic examples of the two extreme situations of coordination, the fully centralized and the distributed one, so rare? In relation to the first case, we have some historical examples in army organizations, where it is easy to see that a fully top–down hierarchized structure is extremely fragile because of its inability to react to external changing circumstances. In the latter, to my knowledge there are no historical examples of economic organizations in which the design of the new division of labour is a fully decentralized process (a "spontaneous", Hayekian organization).

Instead, a clear example of distributed design is provided by the Schumpeterian picture of "creative destruction", which can be considered as a form of design activity coordinated by the market. Schumpeter's[1] analysis starts from the "circular flow" condition, where producers and consumer are in equilibrium and profits and interest rates are close to zero. These conditions, which describe approximately the status of the economy during the phase of depression within the business cycle, provide new opportunities for innovators. They create new products or new technologies which are "tested" in the market. If the first innovative wave has successful results, the innovations are adopted by imitators, spread through the entire economic system and give rise to a phase of prosperity. New skills, new competences and a new division of labour among firms are created within the economy. At the end of the phase of prosperity the economy exhibits a different division of labour, and a new competences and skills distribution, as the result of the competition among firms and of selection by the market. In consequence the outcome of the process

---

[1]. SCHUMPETER J. A., *Capitalism Socialism and Democracy*, London Allen and Unwin, 1955.

of creative destruction can be interpreted as being the result of competition among different projects, undertaken by different rival firms, which are selected by market mechanisms. From this point of view markets operate as a distributed mechanism of project and design coordination.

This phenomenon has many analogies with the organizational learning process which takes place inside firms, and therefore may be interesting to emphasize the differences and try to explain their nature.

The most relevant difference regards the relationship between cooperation and competition. Schumpeter focuses his attention much more narrowly on the rivalry among firms producing similar goods using different technologies than on the effects of innovation on vertical integration, which presupposes cooperation among firms. This point has been analysed by Williamson in his description of "the fundamental transformation".[1] Within organizations, on the contrary, a high amount of cooperation, based on common knowledge and competence overlapping, is needed to realize new projects: therefore the problem is how the internal relationship must be designed to mediate between the need to maintain a certain degree of rivalry among employees and the need to encourage their collaboration.

Imagine that employees and managers possess – to different extents – the capacities of autonomy and creativity which Schumpeter attributes to entrepreneurs. The problem is why there are not examples of modern business organizations where the design of the new division of labour is a fully decentralized process, and employees do have full and autonomous capacity to innovate: this leads us to wonder which relationships exist among authority, decentralization and control within organization. I will recall some aspects of the problem in the next paragraph, by discussing the relationship between New Institutionalist's and Simon's approach to employment relationship.

I shall not discuss further the features of organizational learning here: the reader is referred to the literature, and in particular to the wide range of works collected in *Decisions and Organizations*

---

1. WILLIAMSON O., *The Economic Institutions of Capitalism*, New York, Free Press, 1985.

by J. March.[1] I limit myself to note that, when considered in its connections with the process of division of the labour, the notion of coordination takes a different meaning from the one implicit in neoclassical economics. For the latter, coordination means making individual and independent decisions compatible; here instead the problem of coordination concerns the relationship between the top–down activity to design new organizational set-ups and the adaptive, intelligent bottom–up reactions by managers and employees, which should give rise to a better adaptation of the organization to the external environment.

6. Opportunism and Loyalty: Feed Back Mechanisms for Adjustment.

In order to define and achieve its goals in an open environment, an organization must be able to redefine its internal tasks, and therefore its internal division of labour. Learning, as the adaptation of the organization to changing conditions in the external environment, thus gives rise to an internal reorganization undertaken in order to pursue pre-established goals more successfully. As we have seen, this process cannot be rigidly hierarchical; but, on the opposite side, we have no evidence of economic organizations characterized by a fully decentralized process of organizational designing. A key point to focus on why the extreme cases of centralized and decentralized designing are not working is how competition and cooperation mechanism works to guarantee the creation and constant exchange of information and knowledge within organizations. The classical feature of knowledge is its partial inappropriability and the impossibility to evaluate it a priori. Within organizations, by consequence, to evaluate the individual contribution to the achievement of a common goal is a very uncertain and "fuzzy" task. In addition, the division of labour and competences give rise to a strong asymmetry of information and knowledge within organizations, and by consequence there is room for opportunistic behaviour and shirking to arise.

---

1. MARCH J. G. *Decisions and Organisations*, New York, John Wiley, 1988.

In the framework of the so-called New Institutional Economics, to prevent shirking, "principals" must design incentive contracts in such a way that the interest of the firm and the self-interest of the "agent" are made to coincide – to a degree.

In contrast with this view, based on the idea to control opportunistic behaviours, let me recall H. Simon' approach, based on the "identification" principle.

Simon claims that the employee enters the firm on the understanding that he will receive a salary in return for willingness to accept authority. Consequently, Simon maintains that enforcement of employment contracts does not present any particular difficulty. In his view, the key element in an organization is the loyalty of its employees.

Let us briefly examine the boundaries between loyalty and opportunism, and compare New Institutional and Simon's approach on this point. If identification exists, the employee who works loyally must not be frustrated in his expectations: therefore the organization must be able to discover able and creative employees and it must also be able to enhance their abilities. Now, what are the typical features of this kind of employee?

If the organization must be flexible, able to learn and to adapt, the most important quality of its employees is not blind obedience to authority but instead the ability to critically and autonomously evaluate new problems, and the ability to deal with disagreements with superiors; this is the typical case of "voice" as analysed by Hirschman.[1]

Thus the following abilities are vital to an innovative organization: a high propensity to evaluate autonomously new situations (solve and frame problems), and a high propensity to resort to the "voice" option when conflicting solutions, or opinions arise in a context of loyalty.

Let me add two qualifications to Simon's analysis of the employment relation: first, employees must not only be able to perform a set of tasks but they must be able to learn how to perform new and unexpected tasks. Secondly, although it is true that

---

1. HIRSCHMAN A. O., *Exit, Voice and Loyalty*, Cambridge (Mass.), Harvard University Press, 1970.

employees accept authority in exchange for wages, such acceptance must be conditioned and active in the sense of the "voice" option. The organization, for its part, must exercise its authority in such a way that it leaves discretionary margins for decision making by its subordinates so that conflicts of opinion can be resolved by allowing the most competent opinion to prevail, thereby reinforcing the identification mechanism.

I wish to conclude with a brief discussion of the limits which creative and loyal behaviour may encounter within organizations and therefore the risk that efficient and dynamic organization may lapse into inefficiency or decline. What follows does not pretend to be an exhaustive analysis; it is only a brief sketch based on the points discussed above.

Consider the situations that may arise in the case of decisional conflict between subordinates and their superiors and when authority is blindly enforced.

In many situations, employees have more specific knowledge of the situation, can evaluate it more carefully then the controller, or are simply better able to frame and solve the problems which arise in ongoing activity. Therefore, if contracts require the blind acceptance of authority in exchange for wages, when disagreement arises over how to perform a given task between an employee and his principal, the conflicting opinions have neither room nor solution. Intelligent employees realize that trying to use the "voice" option will be unsuccessful and that they must therefore accept stupid orders (thereby being frustrated).

In turn, a mediocre principal will prefer blind obedience to voice, and will try to avoid conflicting situations which could reveal his incompetence. He therefore has a strong incentive to reduce the area of common knowledge and competence between himself and employees.

A similar result arises from the behaviour of inefficient employees, who risk being discovered and punished, or perhaps dismissed. Therefore if an employee chooses the opportunistic strategy of minimizing his effort to reach a high standard of ability and competence, and therefore has low competence, then he has a strong incentive to avoid being discovered and will try to evade control by his superiors.

He can do this by using the same strategy as the incompetent supervisor: reducing the area of common knowledge and competence. In situations of a potential conflict of opinions, he will blindly follow orders. Therefore his principal will not receive useful feed-back on the decisions he has taken.

Thus, on the one hand, we have agents who try to avoid control; on the other, principals who do not accept discussion. Both form a group within the hierarchy, a hidden group of mediocre employees who can survive if they are able to increase informational asymmetry or – which is the same thing – reduce the common knowledge area in order to protect themselves. Similar kinds of second-best employees exist at every hierarchical level.

If this group fails to reduce or to avoid controls and disagreements, it cannot expand, and it will survive as a marginal "error" in the process of organizational learning and adaptation: in this case, at any moment, skilful subordinates can challenge incompetent superiors, and able superiors can discover the errors of mediocre employees. Thus an efficient organization applies pressure – and in certain cases also moral pressure – on slack employees and managers. This depicts a possible "virtuous" circle.

Yet the organization may also lapse into decline. As long as the size of the organization increases – despite its internal inefficiency – the dimension of the hidden group expands. Therefore if the hidden group has protected itself satisfactorily, the situation is opaque and it is difficult to detect the causes of and those responsible for inefficiencies. Creative competition thus becomes a very inconvenient way to reach a top position because there is a safe, alternative strategy: joining the second-best group.

Therefore skilful employees may also be tempted to adopt the opportunistic strategy; advancements, in fact, depend on affiliation and obedience, not on skills, results and managerial ability. Opportunism may spread if the expression of voice and loyalty are systematically frustrated. This gives rise to a strong reduction of the areas of common knowledge between employees and managers and therefore reduces the organization's ability to react to errors and adapt to change. Hence if blind obedience to the authority principle prevails over voice, the organization may decline into a bureaucratic and inefficient hierarchy. A vicious circle is thus established.

7. Final Remarks: Virtuous and Adverse Selection Within Organizations.

Summing up, within organizations the virtuous mechanism of competitive selection does not have robust self-enforcing characteristics; under certain conditions, it can be overwhelmed by a mechanism of adverse selection, which can lead the organization toward a very sub-optimal "order" characterized by a strongly authoritarian and scarcely competent hierarchy. The reasons why an adverse selection process can arise have been briefly suggested above: if the area of common knowledge among individuals involved in the realization of a set of common tasks is very restricted, there is room neither for reciprocal control and the prevention of shirking nor for exploiting the positive externalities which follow the emergence of creative behaviour. A tayloristic division of labour, with a rigid separation of competences and a minimization of the common knowledge area among individuals, only apparently simplifies individual activities within the organization: in reality this configuration prevents the working of the most important communication channels among individuals, and therefore prevent, the changes from occurring.

The micro roots of this phenomenon have been clearly evidenced by a large set of experimental results in the cognitive sciences: in particular, as we have seen, the transfer of cognitive skills is limited and requires effort, and organizational routines are partially opaque to individuals.

The fact that individuals have incomplete knowledge of the routines involved in their everyday activity, has a twofold consequence: on the one hand, they can complete it either by recreating its missing components or by modifying it, and therefore even during the execution of standard routines the ability to recreate missing parts is a continuous source for potential micro-innovations.

131

On the other hand the boundaries among different competences and skills cannot be extremely neat and clear, and an overlapping competence area is needed. The smaller the overlapping competence areas among individuals within an organization, as in the tayloristic division of labour, the higher the cognitive effort required to cooperate for the fulfilment of a common goal. Consequently, because of a restriction of the common knowledge and competences area, the relationship among individuals become more opaque, and their ability to evaluate each other's competence and actions is strongly reduced. Now, the difficulty of evaluating the quality and the uses of goods[1] is the most important reason for adverse selection on the markets. The similarities are clear: exactly as happens in markets, where the areas of competence among consumers and producers of a good are totally separated and by consequence consumers cannot fully evaluate goods, within tayloristic organizations individuals encounter major difficulties in evaluating the products and the performances of their colleagues (superiors or subordinates). These difficulties, in an organizational context where the common competence area is too restricted, are therefore the main source of opportunistic behaviours.

In order to reinforce loyalty and identification, individuals (employees and managers) must be rewarded by the mechanism of competitive selection. The organizational design, apart from the awareness of the designers, is therefore crucial to determine the virtuous working of the mechanism of competitive selection, since it may allow a transparent common cognitive area to arise. Only on this basis can conflicts of opinion (and of interests) be resolved with the prevalence of the most competent opinion, the identification mechanism reinforced and loyalty overcome opportunism.

---

1. AKERLOF G., "The Market for Lemons: Qualitative Uncertainty and Market Mechanism", *Quartely Journal of Economics*, 84.

ROBERT MARRIS*

Mr President, I would like to take a few additional moments to congratulate the Banca Commerciale for organizing these lectures and for having generated from Prof. Simon such beautiful lectures. (The response of the audience, which has been very good, is a measure of that.) It gives me great pleasure to say this because I do believe that I was probably the first European economist to publish my understanding of Prof. Simon's original work. And in that context I want to make a little publicity for those of you who have been stimulated by what you have heard from Prof. Simon and would like to read more in a simple form. I want to advertise a book which you can see is written by Herbert Simon (that is not exactly correct, it has three associate authors all of whom are sitting along here). It reprints some classic papers of Prof. Simon which were originally published in somewhat obscure although interesting journals. It also contains the transcript of a rich discussion with Prof. Simon which was organized by Prof. Egidi and Prof. Viale in Torino a few years ago, in which all the people who spake, and especially Prof. Simon, said very interesting things at the rate of about one thing per second. In the book also there are some new papers, some new discussions of the relationship of bounded rationality to economics and business behaviour in the more recent times.

I want to speak about three things that have been provoked by what we have heard.

The first is the future of a more realistic microeconomics, which also means a more realistic macroeconomics, because without a realistic microeconomics we cannot have a realistic macroeconomics.

The second is something about the theory of bounded rationality and macroeconomics, because Prof. Simon has been saying some rather provocative things, which are rather interesting, about his idea of bounded rationality applied to the work of Keynes on the one hand and of Lucas on the other.

Third, and most important for me personally, I want to speak

* Former Professor of the University of London.

about the structure of the economy with respect to the structure of firms: if we were to have a theory that determined the absolute sizes of firms, if we knew the size of the economy we would know the number of firms in it; we would know, in effect, the size distribution of firms and the structure of the economy from that point of view. I happen to know, and Prof. Simon knows, that that type of theory is impossible, but I want to talk a little bit more, from the basis of what he said, about what theory we should have there in its place.

And I will begin by noting that the problem of the degree to which economics is a science which was discussed very well in the lecture, also throws up a problem of great books. It has been a tendency, among the great classic economists, to write books with much verbal description, which is rather realistic and rather pragmatic, combined with formal or mathematical theory which is rather inflexible. This is true of Adam Smith, it is true for Marshall, it is also true, as I will show it in a minute, for Keynes, and it is also true of Pareto. Pareto lectured in Lausanne in the French language, because that is the language of that university. The first of his books where he first introduced the idea of the non-comparability of utility between people which led to his later concept of social optimality, was published only in French, so the verbal justification of his argument has never been translated out of that language. If you go and read it in its original, you will find a low level of rigour; it is just a kind of discussion argument. In the case of the other people for example, Adam Smith and Marshall and Keynes, I hope to show that this contrast between the realistic verbal discussion and the theory is at the heart of many of the paradoxes that we have been discussing.

I will introduce this chain of thought by being a little bit clever and a little bit exhibitionist by taking Prof. Simon's discussion of what we mean by the "Whig" interpretation of science and history, back into its origins in English history.

The word Whig is an 18th century colloquialism for the early English Liberal Party, which was in fact a party of aristocrats, and they traditionally are supposed to believe in democracy, in a constitutional monarchy, in – to some degree – humanism and in particular the Protestant religion. And they contrasted their position with a "Tory" position which would be conservative, believing in an authoritarian monarchy, believing in some sense or other in ideas which we would not regard as democratic, and in many respects would be trying to restore the Roman Catholic religion to the main stream of English society. And the so-called "Whig" interpretation of British history, is of a struggle between those two parties which would continue for 300 years from around the year 1689 – in which the Whigs were always gradually successful; this was (in the "Whig interpretation") a very good thing for Britain, and why we had the Industrial Revolution, Parliament etc. etc. And that was the kind of controversy that Prof. Simon was speaking about when he applied it to the history of science.

I want to say something about that story, whether applied to the history of my country or whether applied to the history of science in the world. In the case of natural science, at least, I believe that the Whig story is essentially true, at least for British history up to the year 1900 I do believe there was a constant progress to more democracy and I happen to hold the view that the Protestant religion was very successful for economics etc. etc. I also hold the view that conventional natural science has been very successful, but to say that we are never learning more about the world as we make experiments in natural science, is absolute nonsense. And I think that Prof. Simon in quoting that thought had the same idea.

The problem that we have in economics and some other social sciences, is a science which is not based on definitive experiments. The reason why there is continuous progress in thought in natural science, is because a bad theory can eventually be absolutely disproved. There was a very beautiful theory about cosmology invented by an old colleague of mine in Cambridge, it was called "the theory of continuous creation", it was a very elegant theory, and it is an attractive theory philosophically. But it really was basically disproved by a single astronomical observation, and once that observation was made no cosmologist was going to support that theory anymore. Now we know that in any science which is based on statistical experiments, however sophisticated, we will never have that kind of situation. Not only is it true in economics;

it can be true in medicine. For example, the evidence that relates cancer of the lungs to cigarette smoking, even to this day, is basically statistical. And so, although that overwhelming statistical experiment was conducted by Prof. Doll, nearly 40 years ago, we still have a regime in which it is legal for people to smoke, even though on the evidence they are as poisonous and dangerous as many things that are completely illegal. And the reason why public policy has gone so slowly in that field is because there is no absolute definitive experiment that settles that mattter once and for all.

This situation has undoubtedly had a major impact on economics, in that we are a particularly bad example of the possibility of theories persisting which certainly do not fit the facts very well. More and more evidence comes that the theory is not a very good theory and yet the theory persists because of ideological or other intellectual properties that it may have. Recently we have seen a beautiful example of this in what the traditional theory of the firm would predict about the process by which one firm makes a hostile merger attempt on another.

That process is conducted, according to the traditional theory, exclusively for the benefit of the shareholders of the acquiring firm. Therefore it should be the case that the statistics should show that the shares of firms which are successful in making hostile takeovers subsequently do well on the stock exchange. And in search of that idea a group of people at the Harvard Business School conducted the most sophisticated statistical research to investigate this question, and discovered that, on the contrary, it was not possible to find any great significant benefit for the shareholders of the acquiring firm. More and more statistical investigations were made and every time they were extended we came to this result. Now, you would have thought that that might have led the whole world to say, "oh well of course the answer is that the motive for take overs is not the traditional ones, but something else, for example it is the increase in the power of the management of the acquiring firm". But no, these research workers said, "of course our theory should have predicted exactly what we see here, because in fact somehow in the market the whole benefit of the takeover has been discounted into the price of the share for the acquired firm". And so the idea that a takeover is conducted for the benefit of the shareholders of the acquiring firm continues despite this result. Now, this is very common in economics, as we know, and Prof. Simon has given us some hints in his lecture of how we should have a more scientific economics, in my opinion he has not given us – shall we say – the operational details of his programme, he has given us suggestions but not the complete apparatus. And one way I think things may develop in the near future – very much in the context, shall we say, of experimental economics, but also in the context of new and recent developments in the understanding of the human brain – outside social science, is that, in the field of cognitive science, there are currently very rapid advances in the understanding of how the biological brain actually works. Of course it is not definitive but it is moving fast. And I believe that it should be possible to create a theory which describes most of the agreed discoveries about the nature of the brain, about what goes on in this part, that part and so on, which would then be set to work to try to generate models economic behaviour and economic decision making. For example consumer theory, must start from some primitive desire for food, or something like that, and yet starting from that very primitive desire for food, we have economic consumers who have very sophisticated capacities for decision making between one kind of food and another, between food and this, and this, and this. So somehow from a very primitive system, which we know to exist, we arrive at a very sophisticated decision making process. And the question of whether that comes to look like what economists assume about the utility function will be something to verify empirically. When we pursue this research further, either we shall find a utility function there or we shall not. We may find another type of procedure for making economic decisions, or alternatively we might find something much more like the utility function that we would expect. One reason why we might find that is because we know that the unconscious brain has an enormous capacity for holding information, and the limitation on computing which Prof. Simon is always pointing out to us, is a limitation on the thinking process of the conscious brain: the conscious brain has to select a certain amount of material for examination at one moment of time, and it is very slow and very capacity limited. But when people make decisions which they cannot quite explain – which they call intuitive – they may be using information from the unconscious brain, they may be using a much wider range of information. And by pursuing research of this kind we may find that the unconscious brain has something more like a utility function. I do not believe that but it is possible. And that is one direction where we could go I think, so that economics could become a more effective and realistic science, more like a natural science. I said in a previous intervention that I thought that, in the last twenty years, it had actually moved away from being scientific, it had become more theoretical, more sophisticated, econometrics had become better and better, and yet I believe economics as such has become, in a deeper sense, less scientific. And I think this is a view that Prof. Simon and I share.

That concludes my intervention on my first topic. I want now to say something on my second subject which is the relationship between bounded rationality and macroeconomics. I happen to hold the opinion (which I actually know to be correct!) that Keynes was very confused in what he said in that book concerning the cyclical behaviour of real wages. At one point he seems to say that in order to have a recovery from the depression it is necessary for the people who are not unemployed – who are employed – to "acquiesce" to a reduction in their real wages. He does not say what will happen if they refuse to acquiesce, for example by indexing their nominal wages. He does not say that in that case the recovery could not occur, and the confusion in those short passages, which occur in about three pages of the book, in my view has led to 50 years of subsequent confusion. But never mind about that, supposing Prof. Simon could be correct in saying that for the Keynesian theory to work, in order to make it possible that there will be depression, depends on the money illusion of the workers, suppose that could be correct (I do not believe it, I believe it is an American interpretation of Keynes) but supposing it were correct, it gives one some uncomfortable problems, because it seems to imply that if the Government could make propaganda that could teach the workers to distinguish between

nominal and real wages, we could immediately go to full employment, and I do not believe that. And nor does anybody else
in this room. And that is the kind of difficulty you can get into
with bounded rationality developed into an explicit theory as
against an obviously realistic description of a process.

Now that is one example and I want now to go into something
of which I am actually even more sure, and this is concerned
with the sizes of firms and with Alfred Marshall. Alfred Marshall published a book from which Prof. Simon was quoting, in
his first edition, in the year 1891, and this contained a theory of
the size of the firm which had two aspects, a static and a dynamic. The static was the famous curve that we know about, the
dynamic aspect was the famous story of the trees in the forest,
and that analogy was that of course firms could be quite small,
they would be below their optimum size, according to the static
theory, and they would grow gradually to a larger size, and he
then said "they grow like trees in a forest". And as he wrote this
he clearly became very excited by the analogy and must have forgotten his diagrams, because he said that some of the firms would
grow and grow, and grow and get more light, and get bigger than
the others and the more light they received, the larger they would
grow and the greater they would advantaged. In other words he
was beginning to describe an unstable system in which some
firms would get larger and larger and larger and others would be
pushed to the ground.

And then he had to stop, because he suddenly realized that
this would mean that his whole economic system was not convex.
So he said of course these ones that are growing as if they would
grow on forever, but they do not, they stop. And why do they
stop? Well, the owner of the firm will eventually get old and
when the owner of the firm is old he becomes inefficient, he must
retire and he must give the firm to his son. His son, however, is
the son of a successful man, and therefore will have been cared
for not by his own father and mother, as poor people, but by a
professional maid, a nurse. The nurse will have been very weak
with the boy, will not have given him a strong discipline, therefore he will not have very much motivation and therefore when
he succeeds into his father's business, he will lack motivations

and the business will go downhill. Now, this little piece of amateur sociology was the entire theory in the 1891 edition. Now we come to the 1912 edition, when he told the same story, but he removed the nurses (he must have realized that they were not such a strong basis on which to found such an important theory) and he said of course, it is possible that some firms will grow large and then they will stagnate, they will not necessarily die; this is because we have now invented the joint stock company, and the wording he used was to say that the joint stock company was not very efficient but was typically rather slack, but they had things about them that would make it less likely that they would go down. And that was the wording of the 1912 edition. And it was a later edition, from which Prof. Simon was quoting, probably the 1920's edition, when you can see he changed the wording again because now he looked around the world and he saw many, many successful persistantly growing joint stock companies. And what did he say about them now? He still could not bring himself to say that they might grow, grow and grow, or that they were efficient; all he said was "well the management are not so fraudulent as we might have feared they would be" and left it at that. So the whole thing was left open.

So we see that the words were changing, but what was happening to the theory? Well the theory that survives from Marshall in every elementary textbook of economics today, is the theory of that horrible curve that goes up and down like a toilet pipe, for which in the long run there is no theoretical or empirical justification whatsoever. Nobody has yet produced any empirical evidence that there is any upper limit to the size over which a firm could be efficient. These firms like IBM and General Motors, which are in trouble today, are in trouble because their size makes them not easy to adapt to crises and to big changes, but in their high time they were very, very, very efficient. IBM has completely changed itself, at least twice in its history, but this time may be the fatal one. But maybe not. General Motors was extremely efficient in producing cars, but it was not very efficient moving into another world altogether. And you cannot find in any data a robust negative correlation between the sizes of firms and their profitability.

On the theoretical side I am satisfied that those who worked in this field in the 1960s including Prof. Simon created the apparatus for showing why it would be that firms, as administrative organizations, expanded; there is no special reason why they should become more inefficient. And I thought that was the end of the matter and now we should be interested in something different which is the dynamics rather than the statics of this problem. But no, it turns out as I have gone recently back into the literature of agency theory, that the agency theorists are still attempting to take from Coase the idea that there could be an upper limit on the size of the firm. In the famous article that has been quoted over and over again today, Coase argued that as a firm expanded it was in effect making more and more use of what he called the advantages of internal coordination and it would be comparing the costs and benefits of that type of coordination against the "costs" of using the market – the so-called transaction costs. He wrote a sentence which implied two curves, the marginal cost of internal coordination and the marginal transactions costs. He implied they would eventually intersect, thus determining the optimum size of the firm.

Coase did not actually give you a reason why these curves would have a particular shape. It was just some words, but these words had the most dramatic effect on the economics profession, as we can see. And in fact it turns out that what must be happening is that as the firm expands it is bringing in more and more managers for which there is a motivation problem. This is before we come to the sophisticated stories we have heard from Prof. Egidi. And as we bring in more and more managers who are not owners but who are professional managers, where there is a problem of motivation, the system will become more inefficient. But the problem is that as we bring in more and more managers of this type, let us imagine that each one that we bring in has a constant level of inefficiency, there is no obvious reason why this effect should be what we call in economics an increasing effect. If so the firm can expand indefinitely with a constant unit degree of inefficiency and provided there is a market that it can create for its activities which is good enough to compensate for that, there is no limit to its size. And this is extremely important, and I am

absolutely certain that this is right, and I think you will find that
if you look through all the agency theory literature, claims that
that theory has determined the size of large corporations are not
born out in the literature itself. There is a famous paper by Profs.
Jensen and Meckling in 1976 in which they admit that this is the
case and state that in future they will publish articles in which
they would attack the problem. But I don't think that these articles have ever been published. So where do we go from there?
The right approach in my view is to build on the idea that Prof.
Simon was talking to us about in his lecture when he spoke of
Gibrat and of the general work of people workingon the theory
of the size distribution of firms who were publishing in the 1950s
and 1960s. These people were Peter Hart and Sigmund Prais in
England and Herbert Simon and his associates such as Dr Ijiri in
the US, both working in a similar theoretical direction. And they
say that if you imagine that under these conditions of constant
static returns to scale a firm can expand indefinitely so long as it
expands all its inputs together in proportion, then the question is
not the level to which it expands but the rate at which it expands.
And it is very easy to see that what we are talking about here, over
and over again, is the proportional growth rate of firms, when
everything in the firm expands proportionallly – assets output,
profits, stockmarket value. And the suggestion is that the proportional growth rates of firms are something stochastic which
are the result of all kinds of accidents of commercial life, and if
that is the case it turns out as a very simple piece of theory that if
the growth rates of a population of objects proportional are, in
other words that the rate of change of the logarithms of their
size, shall we say, are normally or roughly symmetrically distributed, then what you will end up will is something which is approximately symmetrically distributed in the logarithms, you
will get either a log normal or a Pareto distribution. Further-
more, unless we introduce some other assumptions, we will find
that the variance of these distributions of logarithms increases
linearly through time. It is not required that large firms are
efficient or inefficient, or anything like that, it is the chance that a
large firm will grow proportionately next year by a certain
amount equal to the corresponding chance of a small firm; that

is all we need. Then set this process going and the variance of this distribution, logarithmic distribution, increases linearly in time, this is the Gibrat theory. And that means that in fact the degree of concentration is increasing through time. We can modify this model by putting into it the possibility that in fact the very large firms are less likely to grow in the next period, there is some negative correlation between absolute size and growth rates, or we can put in a positive correlation. This is an empirical question and if we do that we have a model in which either the system grows asymptotically to a constant level of concentration, or it grows with linearly increasing concentration or it explodes. We can have these three models.

Now this story will then be affected by three things: by new firms entering the population, by small firms that have become big, and also by takeovers. If a firm of large size takes over two firms of medium size, and that is the typical action, then the effect of takeovers is to increase concentration, so you need a model of that. If you combine all these things together you can model the whole process. So what we would then see is not a picture of the absolute sizes of firms but a picture of the rates of change of size generating an absolute size distribution.

So the structure of the economy that we see, sort of static because it may have settled down to a constant concentration, is not the result of a static theory about the individual firm but of a dynamic theory. And the other thing about it which is extremely important is that although we will find that the 100 largest corporations that are taking larger and larger shares, for example of total output, the top firms are not always the same firms, they are changing all the time. General Motors is going to go down, IBM is going to go down, but Apple is going to come up, etc. etc.

Now to my mind all of that is very exciting and very convincing but what was missing from it is that it does not have a theory of the growth of the firm and here I have to say something which is embarassing, because I have recently gone back into this field. I have not found a theory of the growth of the firm which exists in the literature of the last 15 years. I have found theories of the growth of the firm in the literature of 25 years ago, one of which is my own, and I have to say that it still seems better and more effective for the problem we are talking about. I hate to have to report this to you because it is very vain, but it seems to be true and it turns out that – I cannot possibly go into that theory now – if you have a theory of the growth of the firm, it will turn out that the growth of the firm proportionately in the future is very much driven by the accidents of commercial history which determine the return of its earnings on its past investments. In other words, past profits, normalized for the size of the firm, have a very important influence but not a unique influence on the growth of the firm as chosen by its managers in the future. And in some versions of this theory that relationship is linear. Consequently if it turns out that the profits which firms earn on their existing activity are stochastic, which they obviously are, and if for example the rates of return are symmetrically distributed, shall we say approximately normally distributed, which statistically they are, then we have a normal distribution of current profit rates which is generating a normal or symmetrical distribution of future growth rates. So we have a normal distribution in current profit rates generating a normal distribution in the logs of the sizes of the firms in the future. Which is sufficient, I am well aware of that, which is sufficient to produce the entire result that we have been talking about. The basic conclusion is then that if we have a theory of the growth of the firm and we combine it with the original ideas of Herbert Simon and Gibrat of the 50s and 60s, the structure of the economy is not determinant in an absolute sense. That is the reality.

ALDO MONTESANO*

My comments concern the relation between neo-classical economic theory and Professor Simon's research and, therefore, Professor Simon's criticism of neo-classical theory. I would like to state at the offset that I do not consider Prof. Simon's approach a substitute for neo-classical theory, but rather, a complement.

Since the term "neo-classical theory" is rather vague, it is worthwhile identifying right away, even if synthetically, what I mean by neo-classical theory before examining some of its aspects in relation to Prof. Simon's thesis. Neo-classical theory views society as a set of agents that carry out exchange and production. The basis for explaining their behavior is provided by two hypotheses: the first assumes that agents' actions are intentional (or rational), the second, that their actions are compatible (that is, they can be carried out so as not to generate signals that induce agents to change their choice at the moment that the decision is taken). We have an equilibrium if all the actions are rational and compatible. Neo-classical theory describes – explains – economic reality by means of this notion of equilibrium, or in other words, neo-classical theory interprets the observable acts of exchange and production as rational and compatible actions.[1]

The rationality of agents' behavior plays an important role in Prof. Simon's research (see, for example, Simon, 1976, and also many other works by Prof. Simon on this subject). In my opinion, at least three types of rationality are relevant to neo-classical theory. The first type defines neo-classical theory as a rational theory, that is, nomological-deductive (generally speaking, like rational mechanics in physics). In particular, agents' behavior is determined by means of reasoning and calculation. However, such a theory certainly does not require that the objects under study are able to solve the calculations necessary for determining their behavior. For example, in mechanics, the motion of a missile is described by the solution of a differential equation and a body is in equilibrium if its potential energy is at a minimum.

* Università Commerciale Luigi Bocconi, Milano.
1. MONTESANO A., La struttura logica della teoria dell'equilibrio economico generale, in *Giornale degli Economisti*, 41, 1982, pp. 431-440.

Nonetheless, this does not require the missile to solve complicated calculation and that the body be able to pursue an optimum. Therefore, if the economic theory is rational, it could be that the behavior of the agents is optimized and described by the solution to complicated calculations without the necessity of presuming a particular ability on their part.

The second type of rationality refers to the agents (the first referred to the theory) and consists of the hypothesis that the agents' actions are intentional, or that the agents have a choice criterion. In other words, we assume that the agent chooses between the alternatives he perceives as possibilities, the ones he prefers (however, there is not necessarily a unique choice and the chosen alternative is not necessarily compatible with the choices of the other agents, in which case the actions are not in equilibrium and we would proceed with an adjustment process). Therefore, in neo-classical theory, the choice criterion consists of following a preference ordering that is often represented by means of a utility function. (It should be noted that a preference ordering can be represented by a utility function if some regularity and continuity conditions are satisfied[1] – and that it does not absolutely imply that the agent is selfish).[2] Utility maximization is, therefore, only one way, introduced by economists, to describe the behavior of a rational agent which is such because he/she has a choice criterion. In this framework, the irrational agent is the one who acts without a criterion. The economist should thus describe his behavior as casual (moreover, even a rational agent can deliberately choose to act randomly). Another irrational situation (or better, an a-rational situation) occurs when the agent cannot choose because he/she has only one alternative, that is to say, the assumed choice is missing: then, his/her behavior is determined by circumstances alone, as for inanimate objects in physics (this approach is often followed in biology and even in sociology).

1. DEBREU G., *Theory of Value*, New York: J. Wiley, 1959, p. 56.
    BARTEN A. P. and BÖHM V., *Consumer Theory*, in ARROW K. J. and INTRILIGATOR M. D., eds., *Handbook of Mathematical Economics*, vol. II, Amsterdam: North-Holland, 1982, pp. 388 and 381-429.
2. PARETO V., *Manuel d'économie politique*, Paris: Giard, 1909.

The third type of rationality refers to agents' preferences. This requires that not only the agents have a choice criterion and therefore, preferences (as required by the second type of rationality) but also that the preferences have certain characteristics that economists define as rational. For example, some economists believe selfish preferences are rational; many economists, in the analysis of risky choices, believe that the preferences on lotteries described by the von Neumann–Morgenstern utility functions are rational; still, various economists hold as rational preferences that incorporate expectations of the type referred to as rational. Nevertheless, besides the arbitrariness in considering some preferences rational rather than others (for example, for some economists, including Allais, it is in no way irrational to not conform to the expected utility theory), the rational specifications of preferences has substantially a practical objective. The economist is incapable of describing and reaching relevant results on the behavior deriving from any preference whatsoever and concentrates his/her analysis on some types of preferences that he/she considers more interesting, those that show rationality. In other words, it is the limited capacity of the economists' analysis (his/her limited rationality in the words of Prof. Simon)[1] that pushes him/her to concentrate attention on behavior which is derived from preferences considered rational. Often a normative content is given to these rational preferences, imagining that they are objectively better for the agent under consideration and such that he/she would adopt them if he/she could recognize them. We note that the agent's behavior is often determined by way of complicated calculations when we assume rational preferences: the calculations, however, are performed by the economist to describe the behavior of the agent on the basis of an assumption made for practical reasons that serve in specifying the preferences, while the agent limits himself/herself to choose that which he/she prefers. Let's consider for a moment the neo-classical theory of the consumer as described by Debreu for the case of uncertainty. We observe that there is only a preference ordering

1. SIMON H. A., "From Substantive to Procedural Rationality", in LATSIS S. J., ed., *Method and Appraisal in Economics*, Cambridge: Cambridge University Press, 1976, pp. 129-148.

on the vectors of goods, among some of which the agent chooses the preferred (in this representation the goods are qualitatively defined even in relation to the state of the world, so that we assume preferences on actions without determining this on the basis of the preferences on the consequences of the actions and on the probabilities of the states of the world). Moreover, it has been experimentally observed that the choice of many agents does not follow expected utility theory (which is considered rational by many economists even if it is not implied by Debreu's consumer theory). Except for the "frame effects" (which are more interesting for psychologists and swindlers than for economists), there are reasonable preferences, for example those which lead to the Allais' and Ellsberg's paradoxes, that are in contrast with expected utility theory. New theories have been set up, even axiomatic (for example, expected utility theory with rank dependent probabilities, expected utility theory with non-additive probability, and others), which generalize expected utility theory. This is a case in which the experimental results have stimulated the theory, and although they provide a description of the more general preferences of expected utility theory, they are still a specification of preferences.

Of the three types of rationality indicated (i. e., the rationality of the theory, the rationality of the agent and the rationality of the agent's preferences), neo-classical theory requires the first two (the first because neo-classical theory is nomological-deductive and uses, therefore, reasoning and deduction, the second because it assumes that agent's actions are intentional), while the third type of rationality is not indispensable but is sometimes introduced for convenience. Therefore, the criticism applied to some assumptions of preference rationality (much of Prof. Simon's criticism is of this type) pertains only to these assumptions, not to neo-classical theory.

While the criticism of the preference rationality assumptions accuse neo-classical theory of being too demanding, other of Prof. Simon's criticism accuse neo-classical theory of offering too little, or of showing trivial laws (like the downward sloping of the demand curve) or of being rudimentary (like the theory of the firm). In this respect, the presence of trivial laws is not in and of itself a criticism (even in physics we do not need to introduce the theory of universal gravitation for stating that apples fall from trees). Moreover, neo-classical theory does not only determine that the demand curve is generally downward sloping and that supply is increasing, it also arrives at non-trivial results: for example, to determine that if individual demand for a good is increasing with respect to income, then it is surely decreasing with respect to price (while it could be increasing in the opposite case); that demand for an input of production is decreasing with respect to the price while its supply could be increasing or decreasing; etc. In addition, it is able to determine, once the circumstances are specified, i.e., the "data" (population, preferences, technology, social organization, etc., which are not subjects to be determined by the theory), the values of the economic variables, that is to say, the actions of the agents. Finally, since the aim of neo-classical theory is the representation-explanation of an economy with decentralized decision-making, it is not immediately clear if and under what conditions this type of economy is efficient. The neo-classical notion of Pareto-efficiency is exactly the agents' instrument for evaluating the state of the economy. In exchange theory an economic state is Pareto-efficient if its agents are satisfied with their contracts, that is to say, they do not think they can extract advantages by potential (but not admitted) recontracting: for example, a monopoly equilibrium with one price is not Pareto-efficient since the agents could reach a preferred allocation with further trades at lower prices. The notion of Pareto-efficiency, in the general form described here, holds also in the case in which the agents have preferences (incomplete preferences) that induce them to behave satisfactorily (in the sense given to this term by Prof. Simon): in the example, a pure monopoly equilibrium with one price is not Pareto-efficient only if further trading takes place whenever the agents are given the possibility.

We must keep in mind that neo-classical theory, like all other theories, is not the theory of the world. It allows us to explain some events, and not others. It does not explain, but at most provides some direction about what individual preferences are and their changes in time, the total population and its composition, the social organization and the market regime, the distribution of wealth, technical progress, etc. It does not provide, among other things, a theory of the firm. Neo-classical theory includes a production theory, but not a theory of the organization where production decisions are made. The firm is not the production unit of the neo-classical theory (even if this is sometimes called the firm). The real firm can even produce nothing, but be the owner of goods and of shares of other firms. The distribution of the firm according to size and the evolution of the firm's size over time have no definite relation with the optimal plant size, but are analogous in many ways to the distribution of personal income and to the evolution of personal wealth. If technical progress leads to smaller optimal plant size, neo-classical theory does not require the firm to shrink, but that it adopts smaller plants. Moreover, as with every theory, neo-classical theory is schematic in the sense that it defines the objects of analysis in relation to its purpose, which is the study of the interaction of decentralized decisions. Therefore, every agent is schematized and represented by means of a preference ordering and a power of action (endowment and technology). In this view, the other characteristics are negligible details. (At the same time, in celestial mechanics, the planets, including Earth, are points of a certain mass, position and velocity. All the rest, the oceans and continents and humanity itself, are negligible details.)

The inability of neo-classical theory to provide reliable forecasts is deep-rooted in itself, and depends substantially on the fact, already mentioned, that it is not a theory of the world and that movements over time of economic variables also depend on the development over time of variables (population, technology, preferences, social organization, etc.) that are not objects of the theory. Moreover, with this in mind, the dynamics are not a result of intertemporal expectations and plans of action, as Prof. Simon would have one believe, but rather, these are more the effects of the dynamics. In any case, that is to say, for every theory, the future, to a large extent, is unforeseen. It is the same in physics (at least for Heisenberg's indetermination principle) and this is even more true in economics. For example, man's liberty allows for the falsification of predictions and it is logically impossible to forecast the theories which will prevail in the future (while in the future, the actions depend upon the theory of the moment).

Nonetheless, this does not mean that I do not appreciate Prof. Simon's research and suggestions. On the contrary, I believe they are particularly useful for neo-classical theory. In fact, in the last forty years the axiomatic approach prevailed which focused attention on the formal aspects of the theory, neglecting other important aspects, among which economic reality itself. Moreover, the purpose of economic theory is not only to describe, explain reality, be it purely approximately, so that reality must be taken into consideration, but the observations of the real world and the sciences bordering on economics also provide for what in neo-classical theory is called "data". Otherwise, if "data" must include whatever or, at least, a vast multiple of "data", the results of the theory become generic, able to provide, and not even always, only qualitative laws. Prof. Simon's approach has the merit of examining reality in order to identify, in terms of neo-classical theory, which "data" prevail (for example, which preferences and decision-making processes, which types of organizations, etc.) and to seriously consider the bordering sciences.

In conclusion, I do not believe that the approach set forth by Prof. Simon is substantially in contrast with neo-classical theory, but that it probes very useful areas neglected by the current neo-classical theory. As I previously mentioned, I do not agree with many points in the part of Prof. Simon's lessons that criticize neo-classical theory (maybe because I share a different view of neo-classical theory), but I agree with the proposals he makes; I agree that human behavior is the expression of a limited rationality, that the study of procedural rationality is both important and interesting, that organizations are relevant social structures and worthy of investigation, that we must deal with the real world and the other social sciences, experiment and investigate agents' behavior, etc. But I do not believe that all this opposes neo-classical theory; I believe the opposite, that it is a necessary complement.

RICCARDO VIALE*

1. Simon: A Realist and an Empiricist

In his historical analysis of the economic rationality concept, Simon rightly espouses what he calls the moderate approach: which means not viewing posterity from the heights of contemporary science's success, but identifying with posterity's cultural and social outlook to understand the reasons for *its* success. The reasons why Simon makes this choice are, first and foremost, because the concept of scientific progress as an accumulation leading to truth is relatively untenable, and, above all, because it enables him to use the theoretical lens of bounded procedural rationality to stress how, in some cases, the trend has been one of descension from, rather than ascension to, economic classics.

If we analyse theses connecting motions in greater detail, we may be able to understand how Simon's concept of bounded, procedural rationality is positioned, and what implications it has for economic actor theory.

The first differentiation is to be found in the ontology of the economic actor concept. Does it refer to the general characteristics of the agent, or does it simply single out the functions of the actor who is present in economic contexts? Or, to put it another way, does it describe the real man or only a part of him specialising in economic interaction? If we think back to two of the founding fathers of economic theory, Adam Smith and John Stuart Mill, the difference is clear. In Smith's view, man's self-interested conduct, the object of economic study, was not aimed solely at increasing his pecuniary wealth, but rather at sentiments such as honour, ambition, social esteem, love of dominion and so on – themes of psychological study; Mill, instead, saw it as a hypothetical exemplification isolating a select set of the functions, such as the maximisation of wellbeing and the desire for leisure time, which underpin economic behaviour. *Homo oeconomicus* is thus an abstraction of only a part of human conduct, not of the

* Università degli Studi, Milano.

whole. This "fictional man" differs from the real man proposed by other authors, such as Neville Keynes, according to whom the economic actor is not an abstraction of a specific part of behaviour, since self- interest and the pursuit of subjective utility are pervasive and predominant over other forms thereof, such as altruism and solidarity.

In this conflict, the realistic position would appear to enjoy clear predominance in most of modern and contemporary economics. But the question is: what kind of realism are we referring to? How can the economic actor theory be generated from the characteristics of the real man? One way would be to construct generalised psychological functions that are significant for economic action: this is the way suggested by Hutchinson[1] and by bounded rationality theory. The other is to use intuition or introspection to separate a limited number of principles which govern the behaviour of the real man, and which characterise him as *homo oeconomicus*. This is the way followed by virtually all economic theory from Senior onwards, and the one which characterises the neoclassical global rationality concept. Its aim is to describe the economic agent in terms of a general behavioural principle, that of maximisation and individual utility functions.

These characteristics are introduced by a somewhat "unrealistic", superficial analysis of an extremely limited psychological nature, that of the aims-desires-action triad. Moreover, the psychology adopted is not scientific at all but, rather, of the common-sense, folk variety. The outcome of this supposedly "realist" formulation is thus not all that different from Mill's antirealist or "fictional" version.

Corresponding to this antithetical construction of *homo oeconomicus* is the bifurcation of global and bounded rationality, which is accentuated in the second differentiation, that of the epistemological and methodological basis for actor theory. Once they have been introduced, are the principles which characterise the economic agent aprioristic and unfalsifiable, hence empirically uncontrollable, or are they, instead, falsifiable, control-

---

1. Hutchinson T. W., *The Significance and Basic Postulates of Economic Theory*, New York: August M. Kelley, 1938, reprint 1965.

lable and, in the final analysis, corrigible? The first is, of course, the epistemological option which prevails in economics. It does not matter how assumptions are introduced – whether by observation, instrospection or intuition or completely hypothetically – but once they have been, they are turned into aprioristically unfalsifiable truths. This type of apriorism is to be found in many authors, such as Robbins, von Mises and even Friedman[1], according to whom, indirectly and paradoxically, it becomes important for a hypothesis to be descriptively false in its fundamental assumptions. What counts most is its predictive capacity.

This takes us to the methodological differentiation of empiric scope and control capacity of hypotheses in economics, which gets to the heart of the realism-antirealism diatribe in economic actor theory. Leaving aside the extreme apriorism of classical economics, which is concerned not so much with controlling theory's predictions as with its *ad hoc* application to reality, we can single out two forms of relationship with empiric data. The instrumentalist form considers economic actor theory as a "black box", introduced hypothetically and judged acceptable as long as it produces correct predictions. Whenever anomalies occur, the outer belt of auxiliary hypotheses might protect the hardcore of fundamental assumptions, unless this leads – to use Lakatos's term – to "degenerating problem-shifts"; that is, to a decrease in empirical content. In this case, it is necessary to replace the theoretical core with other hypothetical assumptions. This formulation, which we might link to Friedman's, differs from the empiricist position of Hutchinson and Simon, who also consider empirical research as a way of helping to perfect and improve fundamental assumptions – the theoretical core – insofar as it makes the latter correspond increasingly to reality.

These methodological desiderata are very different from the reality of contemporary economics. Whereas, in principle, the leading neoclassical economists declare their willingness to sacrifice basic assumptions when faced with falsified predictions and degenerating problem-shifts, in practice, contemporary

1. FRIEDMAN M., *Essays in Positive Economics*, Chicago: University of Chicago Press, 1953.

economics is very close to the "classical" approach, well represented by John Stuart Mill, which is, instead, prepared to use the *ceteris paribus* condition to the bitter end specifically to neutralise every anomaly. Simon's procedural and bounded rationality theory thus differs sharply – empirically and realistically – from the apriorism and *ad hoc* conventionalism of much of past and contemporary economics.

2. *The Normative Aspect of Bounded Rationality:*
a Naturalist Quasi-Fallacy

What are the implications of this sharp realist and empiricist characterisation? Let us analyse the concept of rationality in greater depth. It may be broken down into three parts, each corresponding to a stage in the decision-making process.[1] The informative process provides the agent with more or less accurate evidential data, which are then represented and memorised ("perceptive rationality"); through forms of logical and probabilistic reasoning, the decision-making process infers the possible action from the information (decision-making rationality); and implementation processes transform the potential action, more or less accurately, into the real action (rationality of the action). Decision-making rationality may, in turn, be broken down into two forms of rationality: cognitive rationality, which concerns the processing of available data to define the agent's expectations of himself and the surrounding environment, and instrumental rationality which, on the basis of these expectations, seeks to select the most appropriate action. Perceptive and decision-making rationality correspond to Simon's procedural and bounded rationality.

The first problem arises when we address the at once descriptive and prescriptive character of Simon's rationality concept. The old dilemma of positive or normative economics has "jumped with its feet together" insofar as he commits the

---

1. VIALE R., "Cognizione e razionalità delle credenze nelle scienze sociali", *LUISS-Quaderni del Centro di Metodologia delle Scienze Sociali*, Roma, 1991.

naturalist fallacy of asserting that bounded rationality corresponds to the empirical theory of cognitive decision processes.

Simon writes that "People have motivations and use reasons (well or badly) to respond to these motivations, and to reach their goals". In this context, "well or badly" signifies the use or otherwise of the best means available – the best heuristics, for instance – instrumental to reaching a given goal. It is thus possible to judge a decision-maker's rationality normatively through a set of criteria for assessing the effectiveness or efficiency of processes used to achieve a given objective. This set of criteria derives, first of all, from the empirical study of the various general weak and strong problem-solving heuristics, and from the identification of specific techniques and methodologies successfully applicable in the particular type of problem space in a problematic area.

Plainly, the identification of prescriptive with descriptive is unsatisfactory, but a key role is played by the epistemological concept of rationality's instrumental value, which is tacitly added as a key to assessment of the actor's decision. Hence, Simon's naturalist theory whereby procedural rationality corresponds to the empirical theory of cognitive decision-making does not hold. It is necessary to add the prescriptive attribute of "instrumental".[1]

---

1. In contemporary epistemology, the other two most important attempts to justify rationality empirically – the evolutive and "reflective equilibrium" attempts – entail a number of drawbacks.

The first sets out from the premise that, in evolution, natural selection is discriminatory, favouring the emergence of organisms that tend towards genotypical optimality. Hence man's present cognitive apparatus, the fruit of a million years' evolution, is very close to optimality in its reasoning and inferential capacities. This thesis is based on a simplistic interpretation of evolutive mechanisms: the latter are represented not only by natural selection, but also by genetic drift, migration and differential mutation rates, which may also lead to the stabilisation of negative phenotypical characteristics.

Moreover, in natural selection there are phenomena, such as pleiotropy, heterozigotic superiority and meiotic drive, which select less adaptive phenotypes than those potentially available. Besides, even if evolution always tended towards optimality, for it to justify rationality empirically we would have to demonstrate that inferential capacities are necessarily determined by the genome, and that inferential rationality increases individual fitness on a biological and social level. Neither claim appears plausible.

The second epistemological thesis is that of reflective equilibrium, introduced by Nelson Goodman (GOODMANN N. *Fact, Fiction and Forecast*, Indianapolis, 1965). How

The problem becomes even thornier if we consider perceptive rationality. In this case too, it is very problematic to assert that it corresponds to the cognitive theory of perception and memory. Perceptive rationality is concerned with how we build the database on which we make our inferences, hence our decisions, and thus refers prevalently to perceptive and mnemonic inputs. If by cognitive theory we were to understand the general psychological modalities whereby man remembers, hears and sees, it would comprises all the errors, contradictions and illusions which systematically cram our daily perceptive and mnemonic activity, and which have been highlighted in recent years by cognitive science. But we would be hardly likely to construct a concept of rationality on errors, illusions and contradictions. If, instead, by perceptive rationality we mean the perceptive and mnemonic modalities of correct and coherent representation of the real world, then we can perform this screening by tacitly introducing two important epistemological and prescriptive principles; that of truth[1] and that of

can we jusify an inferential principle? Through its adequacy to what common sense intuitively regards as legitimate inferences. How can we justify inferences? Through their subsumption by inferential principles that are considered legitimate.

It is from this reciprocal interaction that the test to justify inferential rationality principles may empirically derive.

Despite its undoubted appeal, applied empirically STICH S. and NISBETT R., "Justification and the Psychology of Human Reasoning", *Philosophy of Science*, 47, 1980, this principle has led to somewhat unsatisfactory results, such as the acceptance of inferential principles like those on which the "gambler's fallacy" is based, and conservative basic frequency estimates.

Nor does it seem possible to apply defensive strategies, such as "wide reflective equilibrium" (plus all the philosophical and social principles which govern individual judgement) or "expert reflective equlibrium" (thus restricting the sample to experts in formal reasoning). Perhaps the most tenable position is the so-called neo-Goodman one, which constructs a cognitive theory of the natural processes at the basis of the intuitive justification of inferential principles. This theory might become the test of the latter's acceptability, and the foundation of inferential rationality itself.

This option differs from Simon's inasmuch as the descriptive level is not that of cognitive decision processes, but the metalevel of the cognitive processes underlying the intuitive justification of the principles which govern cognitive decision processes. Besides, the object is not the cognitive capacity instrumentally effective to problem-solving, but the intuitive capacity to justify inferential rules and principles.

1. Traditionally, one of the first prerequisites of rationality has been that of logical coherence not only in terms of beliefs, but also of the logical implications of such beliefs. The prerequisite of the closure and coherence of the logical implications of a system of beliefs contrasts with a series of reflections on the computational limits and cognitive

coherence.[1] In my view, it is, above all, the principle of truth or likelihood, in its various forms of correspondence to reality – a veritable labour of Sisyphus in contemporary epistemology –

performance of the human mind. The point of departure is what Cherniak calls the "finitary predicament" (CHERNIAK C., *Minimal Rationality*, Cambridge, Mass.: The MIT Press, 1986), which characterises the life of man: it refers to the finite nature of biological time and resources of calculus, which make knowledge of all the logical consequences of our system of beliefs impossible. There is also a series of demonstrations by the theory of complexity. In assessment of the computational feasibility of some classes of algorithms, it has been shown that many familiar algorithms require a computational power so great as to be inexpressible by the human brain. For example, as far as coherence is concerned, it has been demonstrated that a system of beliefs containing the conjunction of 138 independent logical propositions, assessed using the simple truth table method, requires an absolutely fantastic power of calculus and amount of time. Since the human memory contains a much higher number of beliefs than 138, it is evidently impossible, in principle, to achieve every prerequisite of logical closure and coherence.

These considerations are accompanied by the many results of empirical research, which demonstrate how man maintains sets of defective, contradictory beliefs. Suffice it to cite Nisbett and Ross's phenomenon of "belief perseverance", NISBETT R. and Ross L., *Human Inferences: Strategies and Shortcomings of Social Judgement*, New York: Prentice Hall, 1980, according to which a belief, even if falsified by emipirical evidence, is often maintained in the long-term memory alongside the new, true belief.

In view of these reflections, the prerequisite of coherence as a characterisation of rationality seems irrelevant. This does not exempt us, however, from seeking to identify criteria of assessment and acceptability of the formal characteristics of our database, and thence to draw inferences. According to our new criterion, it will be possible, with the inevitable variability given by underdetermination, to judge the rationality or otherwise of our inferences and decisions. For example, if we proposed ourselves a pragmatic-epistemic aim such as the utility of truth, the prerequisite of swift, prompt elimination of all incoherences would no longer seem so desirable. A coherent set of beliefs is not necessarily better from the point of view of truth than an incoherent set. It might be a coherent set of false beliefs. Moreover, faced by an incoherent set of beliefs, before eliminating the incoherence, sometimes it is better to have more data to be certain that we are not sacrificing a true belief for a false one, VIALE R., "Cognitive Constraints of Economic Rationality", in H. SIMON, M. EGIDI, R. MARRIS and R. VIALE, *Economics, Bounded Rationality and the Cognitive Revolution*, Aldershot: Elgar, 1992.

1. The problem of the reliability of beliefs has various complications. The first is to understand what is meant by true belief – whether there is correspondence to facts of the real world through some belief-mapping function, or coherence between belief and its implications through feedback with the environment. The first interpretation is a realist one and forms the basis for causal-functional theories of the semantics of mental states (such as those developed by Hilary Putnam, Saul Kripke, Hartry Field, Ned Block, Michael Devitt, William Lycan, Colin McGinn and Kim Sterelny). The second is pragmatist and is well represented by the theory behind the programme of Holland, Holyoak, Nisbett and Thagard (HOLLAND J. M., HOLYOAK K. J., NISBETT R. and THAGARD P. R., *Induction*, Cambridge, Mass.: The MIT Press, 1986), which uses concepts such as "default hierarchy" to construct beliefs and hypotheses about the world on the basis of environmental feedbacks.

which acts as a conceptual stumbling-block in the way of Simon's programme to reduce the prescriptive theory of procedural rationality to the descriptive theory of perception and decision. To reach his objective, therefore, Simon first has to solve the precriptive problem of how and why a perceptive, mnemonic database is correct, and hence acceptable as a point of departure for our inferences and decisions.

3. Some Gaps in Simon's Realism

The second problem we encounter is that of the scope of the realism of the rational actor hypothesis. Insofar as Simon's bounded and procedural rationality seeks to be a realistic representation of human cognitive acivity, it finds its *raison d'être* in the

The second complication is to decide on what bases it is possible to justify truth as an ultimate criterion for assessment of our database. The most convincing response is the instrumental one: if we have true beliefs this improves our chances of achieving other aims, such as happiness and survival. As Stich has rightly highlighted (STICH S., *The Fragment of Reason*, Cambridge, Mass.: The MIT Press, 1990), this is certainly true if we compare true beliefs and false beliefs. The problem is that, at the mental level, there seems to be a vast computational space occupied by states that have no conditions of truth, that are neither true nor false. Albeit non-semantic, these mental states, such as emotions or the subconscious sphere, may contribute to the attainment of other aims such as survival and happiness to an extent comparable to true beliefs. It is also necessary to explore the thesis that to have true beliefs is a sure way of achieving our most important ends, such as survival and happiness. At a social and biological evolutive level, it is possible to demonstrate instead that truth has costs both in terms of internal resources such as time, waste of energy and the limitedness of physical hardware and of adaptation to the external environment.

In the first case, it is possible to demonstrate that a natural selection process may tend to select a less truthful inferential system as a opposed to a more truthful one, insofar as cost-benefit analysis may reveal the first to be more economical in terms of hardware and that the marginal utility of the second decreases as the true information it is capable of processing increases.

As for adaptation to the environment, it is easy to imagine how very prudent organisms which tend to increase beliefs about dangers erroneously – that is to generate many positive falsehoods – may have more chances of avoiding dangers, and hence to survive, than organisms which process a greater number of true beliefs, but also the odd fatal negative falsehood.

It is better to be a relatively unreliable organism, risk-adverse and generating positive falsehoods – as in the belief that a mushroom is poisonous when it actually isn't – than to be relatively reliable, prone to risk but occasionally processing negative falsehoods – for example, that a mushroom isn't poisonous when it is.

hypotheses and knowledge of psychology. The first question we have to ask is: "what type of psychology?". There are almost as many types of psychology as there are psychologists! Although he sometimes seems to leave leeway to common-sense psychology – which seems to me devoid of empirical content and explicative capacity,[1] – Simon[2] naturally enough, favours cognitive psychology, of which he was one of the main founding fathers. Yet, especially over the last few years, the sea of cognitive psychology too has grown increasingly stormy.

As a model of mental activity, Simon uses production systems composed of the condition-action rules which are stored in the long-term memory, and are governed by the programmes which operate in the working memory. This model presupposes a unitary architecture of the mind, a simple structure of the memory[3] and of the control processes which govern the execution of mental tasks and, finally, the assumption that the processes which govern learning and memory depend upon explicit symbolic rules.

Our first critical consideration concerns methodology: since

1. Common-sense psychology is based on the ascribing of semantic content to mental states such as believing, desiring, wishing and so on. The main objection to this type of psychology is that it is chauvinistic; that is, it is incapable of representing the mental activity of persons culturally and cognitively different from ourselves, such as children, members of other cultures, the mentally disabled and so on. When we ascribe content to a mental state, we must compare the latter to our own. We assert that a person is in a mental state – believing p, for instance – if in the same conditions we would have asserted the same belief p. Plainly, this attribution process cannot happen in the company of individuals with a different cultural and cognitive background from our own. This is a conspicuous and serious limitation for a psychology which claims to be scientific. It also has another limit insofar as it is uncontrollable and unfalsifiable as an action theory. It is never possible to check its predictions independently without presupposing the theory itself in the check. Finally, in asserting the irreducibility of the semantic dimension of mental states, this theory is based on a dualist conception of the mind, which seems today to be confuted by the latest developments in cognitive science.

2. SIMON H. A., 'Rationality in Psychology and Economics', in R. HOGARTH and M. REDER (eds), *Rational Choice*, Chicago: University of Chicago Press, 1987.

3. The memory structure contained in production systems (even the most complex ones such as Anderson's ACT; ANDERSON J. R., *The Architecture of Cognition*, Cambridge, Mass.: Harvard University Press, 1983), is too simplified with respect to the latest hypotheses drawn from psychology and neuropsychology, which identify at least five basic types of memory: 1) the central executive system; 2) the sensory store; 3) the working memory; 4) the permanent memory for fundamental skills; 5) the long-term memory for experience and knowledge.

production systems have the unlimited power of Turing's universal machine, their claim to be a general model of mental activity is unfalsifiable by any empirical psychological evidence. Although we may reject a particular production system which simulates a given cognitive function, if we find it explicatively inadequate, it will always be possible to elaborate another particular production system capable of incorporating any coherent configuration of empirical results. Therefore, since the system cannot be confuted as a general model of mental architecture in any empirical research activity, it becomes difficult to accept the hypothesis of their correspondence with mental reality. This is a body blow for the theory's realist and empiricist claims.

The second consideration is a scientific one. The best way to check whether a hypothesis is realist is of course to see at close quarters how reality – in this case, the mind and the brain – is made up. Lately, cognitive science has cast doubts on the scientific validity of the mental activity of Simon's model, which ought to represent the content of bounded and procedural rationality.[1]

One initial doubt concerns the code of mental representations, which Simon considers entirely reducible to list structures. Are we really sure that propositions and, above all, representations in image-form are built into the long-term memory as list structures? Simon himself has recognised that they cannot represent the images' metrical and spatial continuity properties. It is no longer likely, therefore, as recent neurophysiological research would appear to suggest, that the mental image is irreducible, and that it is produced by the activity of the same structure of the central nervous system as visual perception.

A second, and much more important, doubt regards the type

---

1. It is undoubtedly true that any theory on a natural phenomenon is always an abstraction and an idealisation of the phenomenon, hence even a mental theory is different from the mind itself. Moreover, no one questions the methodological utility of computational models of the mind and related programmes for avoiding incoherences, incompletenesses or hypotheses incomprehensible at an intersubjective level. However, the use of such models – production systems, for example – sets out from the uncorroborated premise that the mind is a computational phenomenon like one of Turing's machines. If, in a near future, it was demonstrated that the effective procedures of the mind cannot be simulated by any computer, the principal reasons for the importance attributed to these models would no longer hold.

of mental processing. Research in the fields of neuropsychology and artificial intelligence is increasingly reinforcing the thesis that memory, learning and mental activity in general happen not through the manipulation of separate symbols according to explicit rules as in Simon's production systems, but through the parallel processing of distributed representations created by the fusion of many separate experiences. It is the thesis underlying connectionism and neural networks that represents a raw nerve for Simon. I wonder, along with many other cognitive scientists such as Johnson Laird[1] whether it is not possible to identify a compromise between the two approaches envisaging different levels of representation – a high level with explicit, separate symbols and a low level with distributed configurations – and making conscious processes depend on the manipulation of separate, explicit symbols and unconscious parallel processing of distributed representations.[2]

This proposition is of founding value to the very concept of bounded rationality for a very precise reason. We know that the greater part of mental activity is related to, or controlled by, the emotional sphere and needs. We perceive the form of a well-known face in an unknown person because to it is connected, for instance, to our expectation and desire to meet that person. We memorise sometimes complex recollections at a computational level when they have emotional value, and we persevere in our beliefs, even if they are false, if they are connected with the affective sphere. We learn only a limited series of skills or knowledge in a limited time because the emotional and motivational sphere

1. JOHNSON LAIRD P. N., *The Computer and the Mind*, London: William Collins, 1988.
2. Although a structural correspondence between connectionist architectures and the mind-brain unit does not as yet appear relevant, some experimental results seem to go in this direction. In a recent experiment, Geoff Hinton (cited by Johnson Laird, 1988) established distributed associations betwen words and characteristics of their meaning, and then nullified some of the hidden units used to establish the associations. The result was an increase in errors of interpretation of the various words, rather than a complete loss of meaning of a specific word. Many of the errors consisted of elements of meaning appropriate for a word different from the one previously presented. This phenomenon is reminiscent of the profound dyslexia which is verified in certain forms of cerebral lesion, in which the request to read a word is met with a semantically correlated word. It is hard to imagine how this effect might arise in damage to a system based on structural rules.

allows us to focus our attention on the most significant aspects, and to reinforce our memory of the various procedural stages that are successful. We produce a limited number of inferences and reasonings with respect to the huge quantity that is possible in principle, because it is our needs, motivations, emotions, as well as our pragmatic interests, which direct and select our inferential processes. Finally, even the result of these processes often seems determined by causes in our unconscious emotional life, as studies from Kahneman and Tversky onwards on decision psychology have demonstrated. The fact is that, whereas all this limits and constrains our rationality and, more specifically, the rationality of the economic actor, as Mill and Keynes marginally observed, this important dimension of mental activity does not seem to be given the place it deserves in the psychology underlying Simon's bounded rationality concept. This happens precisely because production systems based on rules and explicit symbols seem inadequate as models of unconscious mental life and mental events such as emotion, which seemingly display characteristics of impenetrability and cognitive holism. It is these considerations which give rise to my doubt about the realism of the human cognition theory at the base of the bounded rationality concept, and the need to improve it and supplement it in the future with models of connectionism, especially when the latter become more representative of the cerebral nervous structure and activity.

I do not believe, in fact, that Simon wishes to shun the epistemological aim of constructing theories to represent reality that are more than mere simplifications, useful only for drawing inferences, as some cognitive scientists and many economists seem to suggest. A non-conventional approach, therefore, ought to prompt a greater willingness to accept hypotheses, such as that of neural networks, which seek to construct a closer correpondence between mind and brain, without detracting from the historical merit of the production systems hypothesis as a useful fiction for studying one part of mental activity.[1]

1. One of the most sophisticated models based on production systems is John Anderson's ACT (1983). It seeks to embrace both memory and learning by combining a bottom–up approach with a top–down one, but it is unconvincing in its explanation of how learning might take place in a production system.

4. A Big Bang in Rationality

In conclusion, I wish to ask a question which may sound a little provocative. Faced by what Quine, in philosophy, has defined as the programme of naturalised epistemology, which for Simon means founding a concept that has always been sharply prescriptive such as rationality in an empirical theory such as human cognition, are we so sure that the moment has not come to question the term "rationality" itself?

It is possible to extract two epistemological criteria from Simon's bounded rationality theory to assess the rationality of our inferences: one is antiutopian, the other consequentialist.

According to the first principle (the term of which is borrowed by Larry Laudan, who applies it to scientific rationality), the question we have to answer is: can a given inference, computation and reasoning be processed in the human mind? If a given inferential and computational model presupposes Olympian skills of reasoning beyond the scope of human cognitive possibility, it may be interesting theoretically, but inapplicable as a criterion for judging man's inferential rationality.

The second assessment principle is the consequentialist one. What type of consequence does this modality of reasoning entail in relation to the aims we have proposed ourselves, and to environmental and contextual constraints? Plainly, in this case the judgement on inferential rationality is comparative: that is, an attempt is made to compare different inferential procedures and to analyse the one which – aims and environmental and contextual constraints being equal – is most effective in achieving the objective. If these are the two criteria for assessing rationality, one inevitably wonders whether the moment has not arrived to abandon the very term "rationality", and break it down into the attributes which characterise an inferential-type human activity effective in achieving the objectives of a problematic context. In drawing inferences, why not break the term down into its attributes of power, accuracy and velocity? This might have a number of advantages: it would adapt bettter to the consequentialist and instrumental character of reasoning activity; it would be more suited to the characterisation typical of the analytical concepts which describe an inferential activity as procedure and heuristics; finally, it would be more effective in expressing the limitedness of time, power of calculus, memory and perceptive reliability, which characterise the activity of the mind-brain unit.

SIMON'S REPLY

My comments here elaborate, with modifications and additions, those I made orally at the session when my discussants presented their papers. There is a great deal of what they said with which I agree, for all of them share the view that neoclassical economics is in need of substantial revision. I will pass over these large areas of agreement with little comment and focus on the rather limited, but perhaps not unimportant, issues on which there appears to be less than full consensus. For that reason, my comments may appear more contentious than the extent of our disagreement warrants.

The individual commentators focused, of course, on different portions of my lectures, but with some overlap. Professor Dematté addressed mainly issues relating to the theory of the firm and to my hypotheses about altruism. Professor Egidi also focused upon the theory of the firm, offering some interesting ideas on the dynamics of innovative organizations. Professor Marris elaborated upon and emended the historical portion of my first lecture, commented upon my interpretation of Keynes, and then sketched the curious evolution of Marshall's views on firm size and growth. Professor Montesano presented the reasons why he believes that the conflict between neoclassical economics and bounded rationality is less sharp than my lectures asserted. Professor Viale first took up some philosophical issues – especially the relation of the descriptive to the prescriptive in bounded rationality – then raised questions about the validity of the particular kinds of psychological theories I have been espousing. Professor Goodwin, whose remarks are unfortunately not available here, took the discussion up to the level of the economy, and commented particularly on the impact upon macroeconomics of new developments in our understanding of nonlinear dynamic systems. (I will include some brief comments on his presentation, even though the text of his remarks is not reprinted here.)

Instead of replying to the commentators in the order in which they spoke, I will organize my replies according to the main topics, and thereby reduce the need for repetition, and I hope, make my position clearer and more coherent.

1. How Much of a Revolution do We Need?

Professor Montesano proposes a *rapprochement* or at least a detente between neoclassical economics and the theory of bounded rationality that I have been proposing. I do not want to declare a holy war aimed at the destruction of everything we know in economics. If I did declare it, you would immediately point out that I myself have published numerous articles within the neoclassical paradigm; for there are several circumstances in which the paradigm provides a very useful framework of analysis, particularly those circumstances where it can be used without making its unrealistic maximizing assumptions.

I have found neoclassical theory especially useful for the analysis of long-term equilibrium when it is plausible to assume that resources will be reasonably fully employed: for example, in my papers on the effects of technological change. These aggregative analyses assume mainly that resources will tend to drift toward their most productive uses as defined by market equilibrium. Under these circumstances, the postulate that aggregate outputs (defined, say, by GNP) will be approximately maximized does not rest in any sensitive way on assumptions of individual utility maximization.

Similarly, at a more micro level, one can with few qualms assume that *(ceteris paribus)* an upward shift in supply of a particular commodity will usually reduce price and increase the quantity sold, and that an upward shift in demand will usually increase both price and quantity. Nothing is gained by deducing these propositions from assumptions of utility maximization rather than simply assuming them; for they also follow from much weaker assumptions.

But let me come now to my disagreements with neoclassical theory, which are broad and deep. Professor Montesano makes an interesting, if not entirely sharp, distinction among three aspects (or "types") of rationality in economic theory: (1) the use of deductive reasoning, (2) utility maximization, and (3) additional requirements that may be placed on preferences. He suggests that much of my criticism of neoclassical theory refers to the third aspect rather than the other two. He also makes the rather remarkable claim that Debreu's equilibrium theory is not utility theory because Debreu employs a preference ordering on vectors of goods rather than "preferences on the consequences of the actions and on the probabilities of the states of the world". This claim is dubious, for there is no requirement on the neoclassical utility function beyond that it be consistent, a condition that is satisfied by Debreu's goods vectors.

I have problems with both the second and third of Montesano's aspects of rationality, and even with the first to the extent that it implies that people reason correctly and consistently from premises that are never contradictory. There is an enormous body of evidence that people often reason incorrectly, even in rather simple matters, and from a variety of partial and incompatible viewpoints (determined by the focus of attention) that make the conclusions they draw at one time inconsistent with conclusions they draw at other times. In fact, it is well known that it is generally easier to alter people's choices by shifting their focus of attention than by influencing their underlying beliefs. The practical strategies of political campaigning are based firmly on this principle, as are most marketing and advertising strategies.

If people are inconsistent in their reasoning, then (the second aspect of rationality) they will not maximize utility, however that may be defined. Kahneman and Tversky, among others, have given ample empirical proof of this. As Professor Montesano points out, economists have tried to deal with these difficulties (and with the Allais and Ellsberg paradoxes) by setting up alternative axiomatic theories, so that "the experimental results have stimulated the theory". Regrettably, they have stimulated theory without stimulating much additional search for the facts of human behavior – without determining, by the kinds of careful observation and experimentation that characterize science, how human beings do in fact make these choices and why the actual choices are not those predicted by utility theory.

So while experimental results have been sufficient to discredit the original theory (despite which, a great many economists seem still to hold to it), they have not generally guided the formation of the new theories crafted to replace it. The intended substitutes have largely been the product of armchair speculation guided by formal rather than empirical constraints. Bounded rationality will not provide a more successful theory of behavior than global rationality unless the bounds are empirically determined to agree with those actually exhibited by economic actors.

So Professor Montesano is correct in saying that I criticize neoclassical theory for being too demanding (i.e., making numerous auxiliary assumptions that are not empirically supported), and also for offering too little (i.e., being nearly irrefutable, because nearly vacuous when not supplemented by auxiliary assumptions). But these two criticisms are not contradictory. A theory should not be so general that it is nearly impossible to find empirical evidence relevant to proving it wrong. On the contrary, a good empirical theory rules out a large number of possible worlds and therefore tells you a great deal about the world that is. The axioms of neoclassical economics, with utility maximization at the pinnacle of the structure, because of their very generality lead to almost no conclusions until you add auxiliary assumptions to them, and these auxiliary assumptions require careful empirical support which, in the current practices of economic theorists, they seldom receive.

But perhaps I am attacking what Professor Montesano does not wish to defend. For he himself, in the last part of his remarks, treats neoclassical theory very harshly. He says that "it does not explain . . . what individual preferences are and their changes in time, the total population and its composition, the social organization and the market regime, the distribution of wealth, technical progress . . . It does not provide . . . a theory of the firm". He speaks of its inability to provide reliable forecasts. Finally, he says he agrees with the proposals I make: that human rationality is bounded, that organizations are worthy of investigation, that we must deal with the real world. If we agree on all of these points (and the other commentators also expressed their general agreement with them), perhaps we need not debate too stubbornly whether or not they are compatible with neoclassical theory. It may be simpler just to redefine what we mean by "neoclassical", and make the necessary (and extensive) changes that are required in the methods of economic research and the relation of theory to facts.

As Professor Viale points out in the first section of his commentary, the contemporary defense of neoclassical theory takes a "black box", instrumental viewpoint that is indifferent to what mechanisms actually underlie economic events. We have no reason to accept Friedman's billiard ball argument, or the bullet that knows where to go although it cannot solve differential equations. The differential equations governing the bullet's flight are not supposed to represent the thought processes of a bullet, because a bullet does not have thought processes and its motion is not determined by thought processes. But the motions of human beings are determined by thought processes and we should not take much comfort or satisfaction from the billiard ball or bullet analogies or other analogies of that kind. If we want a theory explaining how people play billiards, we do not want a theory of perfect billiard balls; we want a theory of what heuristics a human billiard player uses in order to plan and make a (often not quite accurate) shot. These heuristics and actions do not involve solving the differential equations of the billiard board; they involve rules of thumb, and it is these practical guides to action we are trying to discover in order to explain the behavior.

There are large gaps in the theories which I and others propose today to replace neoclassical theory, and that is a valid complaint. There is an old adage that "you can't beat something with nothing". It is up to those of us who think there are serious flaws in neoclassical theory – flaws that can't be remedied by modest repairs – to provide the empirically based alternatives. Providing these alternatives has been a major research goal in cognitive psychology since World War II, but a lot of work remains, in which I hope all of you are going to join us. To build a realistic economics we are going to have to deal with the nature of human thinking, including the aspects of it that were brought up by Professor Montesano and the other commentators.

2. The Economy and Economic Policy

In my lectures I touched all too briefly on macroeconomics, about which I can claim little expertise. Such comments as I made on that topic came up mostly in connection with my sketch of the history of concepts of rationality in economic writings from the time of Adam Smith. But the commentators saw through my ruse. Of course any major changes that take place in microeconomics must have great impact upon our theories of the economy and our recommendations for economic policy. So it was quite appropriate that several of the commentators, and especially Professors Goodwin, Montesano and Marris, raised macroeconomic issues in their remarks.

Professor Goodwin reminded us that if we are to arrive at a picture of the economy that can be useful in talking about economic policy or even in describing the operation of that larger economy, we have to solve problems of aggregation. Looking in the other direction, from the computational standpoint, we have to find ways in which we can explain the dynamic behavior of the system without solving all of the microeconomic equations simultaneously. Throughout his career Professor Goodwin has been concerned with that problem, and has made important contributions to our understanding of how we can deal with a many-sectored economy.

Now in his current work, he is showing what happens when we move from an economy governed by linear equations to one that is non-linear. All sorts of behavior can take place in non-linear equation systems that simply do not occur in linear systems – qualitatively different behaviors. If we are to understand dynamic phenomena like the business cycle, it is not enough to understand individual reasoning or how individuals form expectations; it is necessary to put those mechanisms together and to see what predictions they lead to under the difficult circumstances of nonlinearity. Professor Goodwin, in a recent book on the applications of chaos theory to economic dynamics, deals with the difficulties or impossibilities of prediction with a broad class of non-linear systems. We do not yet know very much (perhaps Professor Goodwin would disagree) about the extent to which, and the ways in which, the non-linear systems of economics are chaotic. Getting the kinds of empirical evidence that would allow us to decide when behavior is chaotic and when it is not is itself an important goal of empirical study and a very difficult one, given the rather slow dynamics of economic systems and the small number of cycles we can capture in our data.

Professor Marris has provided a helpful and insightful explanation of my brief allusion to "Whiggish" history, and has pointed out that in economics we do not seem to have the means that other sciences have to kill a theory when that theory turns out to be wrong in a large numbers of matters. It has sometimes been a little hard to kill a theory in the physical sciences too, for adjusting various auxiliary details often allows it to hold on for quite a while. That was true of the phlogisten theory of combustion; and perhaps we can take that as an encouraging example, because finally phlogisten was replaced by the oxygen theory. Empirical observation demonstrated that the theory of combustion had to take into account the gases that were absorbed and emitted, which the phlogisten theory had ignored. The history of phlogisten suggests that neoclassical economic theory, too, will ultimately succumb to the weight of evidence against it.

In my remarks on the history of economic doctrine, I repeated the frequent assertion that Keynes' found a cause for persistent unemployment in labor's money illusion (and I observed that Lucas found a complementary cause in businessmen's money illusion). Professor Marris points out that this interpretation of Keynes is quite controversial. Whether I interpreted Keynes correctly or not (and whether Keynes himself was consistent on this matter) does not affect the point I was making: that it is impossible to build a neoclassical theory of under-employment of resources without strong auxiliary assumptions (in this example, assumptions about a money illusion) that violate the basic neoclassical axioms of rationality. As in so many other cases, the auxiliary assumptions are doing the work without the help of, or even in defiance of, rationality assumptions.

Professor Marris adds a third piece of interesting and relevant history of economic thought: the gradual development and transformation of Alfred Marshall's views on the sizes of firms. As he shows, the known facts of firm size and growth have long been an embarrassment not only to classical theory (as illustrated by Marshall's evolving views on the matter), but also to its contemporary neo-institutional extension in the agency theory of

Coase and Williamson. None of these theories gives any hint as to why the observed size distributions should consistently conform so closely to the Pareto distribution. Marris shows that this fact is readily explained by combining existing explanations of the steady state size distributions with a growth model based upon a normal and size-independent distribution of profit rates among firms.

3. The Theory of the Firm

This brings me to the remarks of the other commentators on the theory of the firm. Professor Dematté raises the central question of why firms come into existence; why coordination through markets does not suffice. As he observes, my answer to this question has been based on two considerations: the need for forms of coordination not easily achieved through markets, and the possibility of forming organizational loyalties. He suggests, I think soundly, that these conditions should be elaborated or supplemented. First, he points out that coordination becomes a desideratum because of the advantages derived from the division of labor: it is the combination of these two – possibilities of coordination and the division of labor – that makes firms competitive against independent agents in the market.

Second, he observes that firms permit a specialization between employees and entrepreneurs on the basis of their attitudes toward risk. Third, in a world of constant change and innovation, firms facilitate the particular kinds of coordination that are required for designing new strategies. I find all three suggestions very insightful. The concept of coordination and the reasons why it may be difficult to achieve some kinds of coordination through markets are topics that have been developed only sketchily in the literature on the business firm, and Professor Dematté's remarks point to a promising direction for empirical research.

Professor Dematté wonders whether we need to assume altruism in order to explain oganizational loyalty. My first comment would be that whether people sometimes behave altruistically is a question, both theoretical and empirical, that needs an answer, quite apart from its specific application to the theory of organizational loyalty. My papers on altruism have been aimed at showing that, contrary to widespread opinion, altruism is consistent with rigorous neo-Darwinian evolutionary models. Whether or not altruism is essential for explaining organizational loyalty (I believe that it is), altruistic behavior almost certainly occurs with some frequency, and this fact had been thought by some neo-Darwinians to be inconsistent with evolutionary theory. My model shows rigorously that the combination of human bounded rationality and docility leaves room for altruism even in a species that is selected entirely for reproductive fitness.

Returning to the topic of organizations, I do not find Professor Dematté's explanation of how we can have organizational loyalty without altruism convincing. He says that some employees will see that identification with the organization will enhance its success, hence advance their long-term interests. But in the general absence of means for measuring the marginal contribution of each employee to organizational success, and the severe limits on the ability of supervisors to control shirking, this proposal does not explain how the "tragedy of the commons" can be avoided under these circumstances. Each employee will consider his or her own contribution to success to be minor, and opportunism will run rampant. For this reason, I believe that organizational loyalty does not develop and organizations do not work well without sizeable infusion of the kind of altruism I have postulated.

Professor Egidi provided an insightful survey of the multitude of forms that coordination can take, both in markets and in firms. I found myself particularly interested in the way in which he amplified and filled out the model of coordination within the firm, a topic I alluded to a few paragraphs ago. As we continue to form a genuine theory of what happens inside the firm, we see that a key to explaining its construction is achieving a better understanding of the kinds of information exchange that take place, both within the firm and between firms. We must try to understand why it is sometimes easier to exchange information within firms than between them, while at other times it doesn't matter much whether or not the flows of information travel across firm boundaries. To achieve that understanding, we need lots of empirical studies of what actually happens in firms as people try to coordinate, to use common information, to construct common frames of references that allow them to think in some kind of co-operation with each other.

Professor Egidi pointed out that in planning within the firm, shared knowledge is created that becomes an important business asset. Moroever, various components of planning tasks and of knowledge acquisition and storage can be specialized, permitting an efficient division of labor in strategic planning. He also joined Professor Dematté in observing that intra-firm coordination takes on special importance in a "Schumpeterian" world that requires frequent search for and development of new products, new market strategies and new innovations of every kind. In this view, the growth of the modern business corporation goes hand in hand with the acceleration of economic and social change, both as cause and effect.

4. Decision Making and Theories of Cognition

What is thinking all about? Professor Marris speculated on what the unconscious brain does, as distinct from the conscious brain, and Professor Viale raised a similar issue. One should not suppose that the symbolic theories that researchers in cognitive science have been proposing and developing (and which I am urging as a foundation for theories of bounded rationality in economics) are limited to conscious actions. If we look at the models that have been built of human thinking (for example, the EPAM model of perception and memory), we find that they deal with unconscious as well as conscious processes. The extensive modeling of unconscious processes in existing symbol systems that, like EPAM, simulate human thinking refutes the claim that the symbolic approach is limited to conscious processes in any way, shape or form.

Both Professors Marris and Viale succumb a bit to the very prevalent mystique of the human subconscious. In folk psychology the subconscious and unconscious are often supposed to be the places where innumerable processes go on simultaneously at high rates of speed, and it is conjectured that it is to these process-es that we must look for explanations of remarkable human per-formances of the sorts we call "intuitive", and even "creative". But we really do not need folklore, speculations or conjectures about these matters. There is a substantial body of evidence about the actual processes, and that evidence simply does not support this view of the role of the unconscious, which flies in the face of numerous well-known facts.

First, brain processes are slow, not fast: it takes about a mil-lisecond to cross a single synapse connecting two neurons, and numerous synaptic crossings are required to produce a single re-sponse. (Performance measurements show, for example, that it takes at least half a second to do something as simple as recog-nizing an old friend.) These speeds apply to unconscious process-es (recognition processes are unconscious except for their final outputs) as well as conscious processes. Second, the neurological evidence beginning to accumulate from magnetic resonance imaging indicates that responses in even rather simple tasks ex-tend over a considerable period of time (seconds and more), slowly and serially traversing successive brain regions. Third, there is no evidence that mental processes of any complexity, ex-cept those that have already been highly automated or routinized through extensive practice, can be carried out without the fre-quent intervention of consciousness. (The evidence, for example, about the possibility of learning during sleep is wholly negative.) Fourth, conscious processes make extensive use of short-term memory, which has an extremely small capacity and hence nec-essarily serializes activity into a one-thing-at-a-time stream.

These are some of the reasons why there has been a great deal of success over the past 35 years in modeling human mental processes, often in complex tasks at the professional or expert lev-el of competence, using computer programs that are basically se-rial, not parallel. These models show that we do not need massive parallel processing to explain how physicians diagnose patients, how chessmasters choose good moves, how scientists discover laws in data, how engineers design electric motors, how children learn languages, how students use mental diagrams to reason about problems in physics – I could continue the list for several paragraphs. All of these performances and many more have been simulated in real time (or faster) on ordinary digital serial von Neumann computers; and the processes followed by the programs have been matched, sometimes at a time resolution of a few seconds, against the corresponding processes of humans performing the same tasks. The simulations explain both successful human performance (at expert and at novice levels) and human error and failure. The evidence from them continues to accumulate over a wider and wider range of cognitive tasks. Hence, I find it hard to understand what Professor Viale can be referring to when he claims that "lately, cognitive science has cast doubts on the scientific validity of the mental activity of Simon's model". On the contrary, the symbol system hypothesis and the simulations that instantiate the hypothesis are at the heart of contemporary cognitive science.

The success of such simulations matching human data does not deny that the symbol system is implemented, at the next level below, by neural machinery that may be highly parallel in many respects. But for the purposes of understanding human thinking in economic decision making, we do not need to descend to neurology any more than molecular biologists (or neurologists) have to build their theories at the level of the quarks, or even at the level of the atomic nucleus.

Thus, I find Professor Viale unpersuasive when he urges "a willingness to accept hypotheses, such as that of neural networks, which seek to construct a closer correspondence between mind and brain, without detracting from the historical merit of the production systems hypothesis as a useful fiction for studying one part of mental activity". No one rejects the hypothesis that the processes that have been modeled at the serial symbolic level are implemented in the human brain by neurons, any more than anyone rejects the hypothesis that molecules are made up of protons, neutrons and planetary electrons. This does not imply that explanations of thought processes need be expressed in terms of neurons, any more than it implies that explanations in biochemistry need be expressed in terms of protons and neutrons. It is fortunate for us human beings, with our bounded rationality, that the phenomena that science studies are constructed in this layered way so that we don't have to model everything at once or model high-level phenomena at the level of the component quarks. I have discussed the implications of the hierarchical structure of natural (and artificial) phenomena in the final chapter of my book, *The Sciences of the Artificial*, which has been translated into Italian as *Le Scienze dell'Artificiale* (Il Mulino, 1988), and the interested reader can find a more complete discussion of the issues there.

What Professor Viale calls "the production systems hypothesis" (which is usually called "the physical symbol system hypothesis") can hardly be dismissed, as he proposes to dismiss it, either as having only "historical merit" or as being a "useful fiction". It has wholly contemporary merit because it remains the only theory that is able to account for the main features of high-level human thinking and problem solving. After more than a decade of connectionist research, no neural network theory has demonstrated the capacity for simulating human processes in any substantial high-level task resembling those listed above. Nor is there much evidence that the networks of the connectionist theories bear any close resemblance to real neural nets, or their processes to the physiological processes in the human brain. Professor Viale is drafting the obituary of the symbol system hypothesis before it has expired, and long before any successor has demonstrated an ability to replace it.

The connectionist theories have shown their greatest promise so far in simulating processes close to the sensory and motor peripheries of the human system (especially the detection of speech patterns and visual patterns), and that is probably where they are going to play their major role. These parts of the human system are as demonstrably parallel in their operation as the more central parts of the nervous system are demonstrably serial. Without solid empirical success in modeling high-level mental processes, the connectionist promises and claims are just that: promises and claims.

Professor Viale believes that connectionist models may have special value for dealing with visual imagery, with the unconscious and with emotion, three sets of phenomena that he thinks serial symbolic systems are incapable of addressing. The evidence shows quite the opposite. There is a great deal of work going on today on the representation of mental images in symbolic systems, and in fact this is one of the main lines of my own research today, and also of a number of other people, Stephen Kosslyn, for example. Recent research has shown that symbolic systems are quite capable of representing the kinds of images that people use in their reasoning – for instance, the kind of imagery that is needed to understand how Einstein derived the Lorentz Transformation in special relativity, and the kind of imagery that is needed to understand what happens to prices and quantities of goods exchanged in a market when the supply or the demand curve shifts.

I have already said a few words about the unconscious. I see no reason to limit our symbolic systems to the conscious aspects of human activity and they have not been so limited, I can point to all sorts of representations, in any one of the symulations and structures in the simulation models, that refer to unconscious processes.

It is true that research in cognitive science has focused on the cognitive aspect, and has had much less to say about emotion and attention. However, a number of important steps have been taken toward linking the cognitive to the motivational and emotional systems. The scheme that has perhaps been carried farthest is the work of Kenneth Colby, who constructed a model of a paranoid patient experiencing emotions of fear, anger and so on. These emotions, interacting with the programme's cognition, led it to engage in the kind of behaviour that clinicians call "paranoid". Of course, this whole area of our study of the human mind, needs to be developed much further. A theory of economics, of how people make decisions, has to be a theory also of what they take into account when they make these decisions; and we know that attentional mechanisms which are driven by emotions (as in such historical instances as the Tulip Craze in the Netherlands) are a major part of this mechanism. I know of no reason why models and theories of emotions and motivations should be less symbolic than models of cognition.

Are symbolic models, as Professor Viale charges, just "useful fictions"? Because science, as pointed out earlier, is constructed in layers, the symbolic processes used to explain thinking are no more "useful fictions" than are molecular structures used to explain chemical reactions, even though both are (or in time will be) explainable at the next level below. The model of science that regards higher level constructs of this kind as "useful fictions" harks back to a primitive, 50-year old form of reductionism that has long since been abandoned by empiricists. Scientific knowledge includes both theories that explain phenomena in terms of objects and relations at the spatial, temporal and energy scales appropriate to the phenomena, and other theories that show how, at least in simple cases, these higher level objects and relations can be accounted for in terms of more microscopic theories at the next level below. Neither provides an "ultimate" explanation, and neither is more or less fictional than the other. Quarks are neither more nor less fictional than protons or atoms or molecules or crayfish. Neurons are neither more nor less fictional than chess moves or steps in a medical diagnosis.

Professor Viale asks "what type of psychology?" and claims that "there are almost as many types of psychology as there are psychologists!" This will come as news to the vast body of cognitive psychologists who carry on research in this field, for they have been celebrating for some years now a wide consensus about the basic description, at the symbolic level, of the organization and operation of perceptual and memory processes and of the higher-level processes that depend on them. I do not find, in either the standard textbooks or the journals, the Tower of Babel that Professor Viale describes. Instead, I find consistent evidence of a large consensus.

I do not mean to imply that there are no disagreements about the specifics of structure in these theories. That kind of disagreement is the life of science. In my own university alone, at the symbolic level we have research going on in the framework of the Soar architecture, which is the product of my late colleague Allen Newell and his associates; the Act* architecture, which is the product of John R. Anderson; the EPAM architecture, which lies at the core of my own theorizing about perception and memory, and others. (At the network level, we have the PDP connectionist models of Jay McClellan and his colleagues.) The various systems deal with somewhat different ranges of tasks (although all aspire to a future generality and unification), and in some instances propose somewhat different mechanisms for the same task. But the differences here do not represent different "schools" of psychology. They are differences in specifics, which will be settled sooner or later by running experiments that discriminate among the theories. Moreover, mechanisms are borrowed freely from one of the architectures to another. For example, a simplified version of EPAM has been implemented within the Soar architecture, and Soar itself is an extension of the earlier General Problem Solver. This kind of diversity within unity is what we expect to find in any progressive science. It is distinctly not a "war of the schools" of traditional psychology or philosophy.

Beyond my fundamental disagreement with the exaggerated role that Professor Viale assigns to the connectionist models, I find that he also has some serious misconceptions about the nature of the production systems that are used to implement both connectionist and symbolic models. He makes the curious assertion that "since production systems have the unlimited power of Turing's universal machine, their claim to be a general model of mental activity is unfalsifiable by any empirical psychological evidence". This is logically equivalent to saying, "As Newton's Laws are differential equations, that is, partial recursive functions, and as partial recursive functions have the unlimited power of Turing machines, Newton's Laws are unfalsifiable". The propositions we put forward in our psychological theories are not simply that human beings can be described by production systems, but that they can be described by the production system called EPAM or the production system called the General Problem Solver, or whatever candidate theory we advance. These specific theories are readily tested and frequently falsified, I can assure you. They are much easier to falsify than is neoclassical economic theory when it is unaccompanied by strong auxiliary assumptions.

The first fallacy in Professor Viale's argument is in his supposing that because a computer is a Turing machine it can, by definition, do anything a human thinker can do. This assertion will be greeted with astonishment by the many philosophers (and others) who believe they have proved that, because of Godel's undecidability theorems, human thinking, especially "intuitive" and "creative" thinking, cannot be simulated by Turing machines. Professor Viale is misled by the term "universal" applied to Turing machines. What the term means is that such machines can compute any partial recursive function, but nothing else. It leaves unanswered the question of whether what human beings are doing when thinking can be interpreted as computing partial recursive functions, and only that. The physical symbol system hypothesis claims that that is exactly what they are doing. It is an empirical hypothesis, to be tested by seeing whether there are, in fact, forms of human thinking that cannot be programmed for computers. It cannot be tested by proving theorems about Turing machines. The verdict is open, but it has already been shown empirically that many kinds of human thinking, including some regarded as "intuitive" and "creative" can, in fact, be simulated. So far, the answer is in the affirmative.

The second fallacy in Professor Viale's argument resides in confounding the full range of capabilities of a digital computer with the specific behavior it will exhibit when it is programmed in a particular way – programmed, for example to simulate human cognitive processes. The physical symbol system hypothesis is a claim that computers can be programmed to simulate thinking. The claim is tested by running specific programs that have been constructed, in the light of our best knowledge of how thinking proceeds, to match the human processes.

Consider, for example, computer chessplaying programs. Very powerful programs (e.g., Deep Thought) are now competitive with grandmasters, but these programs are demonstrably not supportable psychological theories, for they carry out vastly more computation than human brains are capable of: they substitute "number-crunching" power for human selective heuristics. There are other programs – for example, the MATER program that Baylor and I built and tested – that search for mating combinations in a humanoid way, examining only a few alternatives, but using chess knowledge to select those that are worth examining. When programs are claimed to be psychological theories, those claims can be tested by comparing the step-by-step progression of the program's execution (not merely the final product) against the corresponding steps in the human thinking as revealed, for example, by thinking-aloud protocols and data on eye movements. There is no great difficulty in showing empirically that Deep Thought's processes are not at all like a chess Master's, but that MATER's are. Both programs can run on the same computer. So much for Professor Viale's "body blow for the theory's realist and empiricist claims".

I apologize for my long digression on contemporary psychology in a discussion concerned mainly with economics, but I cannot leave Professor Viale's incorrect claims without comment, and I did not want simply to confront claims with counterclaims. Hence, I have had to go into these matters at a little depth. Readers who want to examine the issues in further detail will have to go to the professional literature. If I criticize economics for too often preferring speculation to empirical testing, I find it equally objectionable to try to settle questions about what psychological theories are viable without close attention to the vast experimental literature of that field, and the match of theories to the empirical data in that literature. We have to get the facts straight before we can usefully carry out a philosophical discussion of theory very far.

Finally, I must address briefly Professor Viale's claim that I "commit the naturalistic fallacy of asserting that bounded rationality corresponds to the empirical theory of cognitive decision processes". He thinks that, because decision making is goal oriented, I identify the prescriptive with the descriptive. There is, on the contrary, no contradiction or fallacy in describing a prescriptive process. The description (by the economist) states what the process is; the process (of the economic agent) prescribes behavior. Describing and advocating are two different things done by two different people.

A theory of bounded rationality undertakes to describe the processes that humans use to reach their goals. The behavior it studies is rational in its intention, but may be far from objectively rational with respect to the adequacy and accuracy of the knowledge it builds upon and the reasoning methods it employs.

To the extent that the description of the behavior is a correct theory, it explains human error and failure to reach goals as well as the fact the people do sometimes achieve these goals. There is no reason why such a theory must "solve the prescriptive problem of how and why a perceptive mnemonic database is correct, and hence acceptable as a point of departure for our inferences and decisions". Fortunately for all of us in our everyday lives, we do not have to store in our heads a correct perceptive mnemonic database in order to achieve a partial, bounded rationality. For that purpose, our actual fallible, gap-ridden memories usually satisfice. When they don't, we experience the unfortunate mishaps to which we humans are so prone and vulnerable. A theory of human rationality that did not explain that vulnerability would not be much of a theory.

5. Conclusion

We can, I think, take today's discussion and those that preceeded it as clear indications that economics today and its empirical foundations comprise a very vibrant field of activity. Conflict, is not absent from this activity, but that is fine: the frontiers of science are often full of conflict. There is a lot of excitement in economics today. Lots of opportunities are emerging for sound empirical work, which can settle some of the controversies that have been discussed here and in the world of economics generally.

I have been encouraged by the degree of consensus we have achieved here on the topics of bounded rationality and the nature of business firms. We seem to have largely agreed that economics needs to take greater account than neoclassical theory now does of the limits on human rationality, and that progress in this direction requires extensive empirical research to determine how people actually go about making decisions: what information they use (and don't use) and how they reason.

We seem to have agreed also that we need to advance our understanding of the business firm, the conditions under which firms hold a comparative advantage over markets and vice versa, and the nature of the loyalty mechanisms that secure some degree, often quite extensive, of human attachment to organizational goals. These are just a few of the issues economics needs to address, with empirical evidence receiving substantially more attention than it has received in the past.

There was perhaps less consensus among us in defining just what economics needs from psychology, and what kind of psychology will provide it. Because this series of lectures was directed at economic topics and not psychological or philosophical ones, my comments on these latter issues have had to be rather categorical. I have stated my views as clearly as I can, but readers will have to go elsewhere for a fuller account of the empirical evidence on which they are founded.

We should not be disappointed that we have not reached final answers. If we achieved that, we would all no longer be employable as scientists, and that would be unfortunate. But we need not worry. We will continue to have these debates, but we will also continue to have a Whiggish, progressive theory of science. What we are debating today is beyond what we were debating 30 years ago, or even 2 years ago. There is progress in science, and there will be continuing progress in the science of economics.

HERBERT A. SIMON'S
AUTOBIOGRAPHICAL SKETCH

I WAS born in Milwaukee, Wisconsin, on June 15, 1916. My father, electrical engineer, had come to the United States in 1903, after earning his engineering diploma at the Technische Hochschule of Darmstadt, Germany. He was an inventor and designer of electrical control gear, later also a patent attorney. An active leader in professional and civic affairs, he received an honorary doctorate from Marquette University for his many activities in the community. My mother, an accomplished pianist, was a third generation American, her forebears having been '48ers who immigrated from Prague and Köln. Among my European ancestors were piano builders, goldsmiths, and vintners but to the best of my knowledge, no professionals of any kinds. The Merkels in Köln were Lutherans, the Goldschmidts in Prague and the Simons in Ebersheim, Jews.

My home nurtured in me an early attachment to books and other things of the intellect, to music, and to the out-of-doors. I received an excellent general education from the public elementary and high schools in Milwaukee, supplemented by the fine science department of the public library and the many books I found at home. School work was interesting but not difficult, leaving me plenty of time for sandlot baseball and football, for hiking and camping, for reading and for many extracurricular activities during my high school years. A brother five years my senior, while not a close companion, gave me some anticipatory glimpses of each stage of growing up. Our dinner table at home was a place for discussion and debate, often political, sometimes scientific.

Until well along in my high school years, my interests were quite dispersed, although they were increasingly directed toward science – of what sort I wasn't sure. For most adolescents, science means physics, mathematics, chemistry, or biology – those are the subjects to which they are exposed in school. The idea that human behavior may be studied scientifically is never hinted at until much later in the educational process – it was certainly not conveyed by history or "civics" courses as they were then taught.

My case was different. My mother's younger brother, Harold Merkel, had studied economics at the University of Wisconsin under John R. Commons. Uncle Harold had died after a brief career with the National Industrial Conference Board, but his memory was always present in our household as an admired model, as were some of his books on economics and psychology. In that way I discovered the social sciences. Uncle Harold having been an ardent formal debater, I followed him in that activity too. In order to defend free trade, disarmament, the Single Tax and other unpopular causes in high school debates, I was led to a serious study of Ely's economics textbook, Norman Angell's *The Great Illusion,* Henry George's *Progress and Poverty,* and much else of the same sort.

By the time I was ready to enter the University of Chicago, I had a general sense of direction. The social sciences, I thought, needed the same kind of rigor and the same mathematical underpinnings that had made the "hard" sciences so brilliantly successful. I would prepare myself to become a mathematical social scientist. By a combination of formal training and self study, the latter continuing systematically well into the 1940's, I was able to gain a broad base of knowledge in economics and political science, together with reasonable skills in advanced mathematics, symbolic logic, and mathematical statistics. My most important mentor at Chicago was the econometrician and mathematical economist, Henry Schultz, but I studied too with Rudolf Carnap in logic, Nicholas Rashevsky in mathematical biophysics, and Harold Lasswell and Charles Merriam in political science. I also made a serious study of graduate-level physics, in order to strengthen and practice my mathematical skills, and to gain an intimate knowledge of what a "hard" science was like, particularly on the theoretical side. An unexpected by-product of the latter study has been a lifelong interest in the philosophy of physics, and several publications on the axiomatization of classical mechanics.

My career was settled at least as much by drift as by choice. An undergraduate field study for a term paper developed an interest in decision making in organizations. On graduation in 1936, the term paper led to a research assistantship with Clarence E. Ridley in the field of municipal administration, carrying out investigations that would now be classified as operations research. The research assistantship led to the directorship, from 1939 to 1942, of a research group at the University of California, Berkeley, engaged in the same kinds of studies. By arrangement with the University of Chicago, I took my doctoral exams by mail, and moonlighted a dissertation on administrative decision making during my three years at Berkeley.

When our research grant was exhausted, in 1942, jobs were not plentiful and my military obligations were uncertain. I secured a position in political science at Illinois Institute of Technology by the intercession of a friend who was leaving. The return to Chicago had important, but again largely unanticipated, consequences for me. At that time, the Cowles Commission for Research in Economics was located at the University of Chicago. Its staff included Jacob Marschak and Tjalling Koopmans, who were then directing the graduate work of such students as Kenneth Arrow, Leo Hurwicz, Lawrence Klein, and Don Patinkin. Oscar Lange, not yet returned to Poland, Milton Friedman, and Franco Modigliani frequently participated in the Cowles staff seminars, and I also became a regular participant.

That started me on a second education in economics, supplementing the Walrasian theory and Neyman-Pearson statistics I had learned earlier from Henry Schultz (and from Jerzy Neyman in Berkeley) with a careful study of Keynes' *General Theory* (made comprehensible by the mathematical models proposed by Meade, Hicks, and Modigliani), and the novel econometric techniques being introduced by Frisch and investigated by the Cowles staff. With considerable excitement, too, we examined Samuelson's new papers on comparative statics and dynamics.

I was soon co-opted by Marschak into participating in the study he and Sam Schurr were directing of the prospective economic effects of atomic energy. Taking responsibility for the macroeconomic parts of that study, I used as my analytic tools both classical Cobb–Douglas functions, and the new activity analysis being developed by Koopmans. Although I had earlier published papers on tax incidence (1943) and technological development (1947), the atomic energy project was my real baptism in economic analysis. My interest in mathematical economics having been aroused, I continued active work on problems in that domain, mainly in the period from 1950 to 1955. It was during this time that I worked out the relations between causal ordering and identifiability – coming for the first time in contact with the related work of Herman Wold – discovered and proved (with David Hawkins) the Hawkins–Simon theorem on the conditions for the existence of positive solution vectors for input–output matrices, and developed (with Albert Ando) theorems on near-decomposability and aggregation.

In 1949 the Carnegie Institute of Technology received an endowment to establish a Graduate School of Industrial Administration. I left Chicago for Pittsburgh to participate with G.L. Bach, William W. Cooper, and others in developing the new school. Our goal was to place business education on a foundation of fundamental studies in economics and behavioral science. We were fortunate to pick a time for launching this venture when the new management science techniques were just appearing on the horizon, together with the electronic computer. As one part of the effort, I engaged with Charles Holt, and later with Franco Modigliani and John Muth, in developing dynamic programming techniques – the so-called "linear decision rules" – for aggregate inventory control and production smoothing. Holt and I derived the rules for optimal decision under certainty, then proved a certainty-equivalence theorem that permitted our technique to be applied under conditions of uncertainty. Modigliani and Muth went on to construct efficient computational algorithms. At this same time, Tinbergen and Theil were independently developing very similar techniques for national planning in the Netherlands.

Meanwhile, however, the descriptive study of organizational decision making continued as my main occupation, in this case in collaboration with Harold Guetzkow, James March, Richard Cyert and others. Our work led us to feel increasingly the need for a more adequate theory of human problem solving if we were to understand decisions. Allen Newell, whom I had met at the Rand Corporation in 1952, held similar views. About 1954, he and I conceived the idea that the right way to study problem solving was to simulate it with computer programs. Gradually, computer simulation of human cognition became my central research interest, an interest that has continued to be absorbing up to the present time.

My research on problem solving left me relatively little opportunity to do work of a more classical sort in economics. I did, however, continue to develop stochastic models to explain the observed highly skewed distributions of sizes of business firms. That work, in collaboration with Yuji Ijiri and others, was summarized in a book published in 1977.

In this sketch, I have said less about my work on decision making than about my other research in economics, because the former is discussed at greater length in my Nobel lecture. I have also left out of this account those very important parts of my life that have been occupied with my family and with non-specific pursuits. One of my few important decisions, and the best, was to persuade Dorothea Pye to marry me on Christmas Day, 1937. We have been blessed in being able to share a wide range of our experiences, even to publishing together in two widely separate fields: public administration and cognitive psychology. We have shared also the pleasures and responsibilities of raising three children, none of whom seem imitative of their parents' professional directions, but all of whom have shaped for themselves interesting and challenging lives.

My interests in organizations and administration have extended to participation as well as observation. In addition to three stints as a university department chairman, I have had several modest public assignments. One involved playing a role, in 1948, in the creation of the Economic Cooperation Administration, the agency that administered Marshall Plan aid for the U.S. Government. Another, more frustrating, was service on the President's Science Advisory Committee during the last year of the Johnson administration and the first three years of the Nixon administration. While serving on PSAC, and during another committee assignment with the National Academy of Sciences, I have had opportunities to take part in studies of environmental protection policies. In all of this work, I have tried – I know not with what success – to apply my scientific knowledge of organizations and decision making, and, conversely, to use these practical experiences to gain new research ideas and insights.

In the "politics" of science, which these and other activities have entailed, I have had two guiding principles – to work for the "hardening" of the social sciences, so that they will be better equipped with the tools they need for their difficult research tasks; and to work for close, relations between natural scientists and social scientists, so that they can jointly contribute their special knowledge and skills to those many complex questions of public policy that call for both kinds of wisdom.

BIBLIOGRAPHY
of Herbert A. Simon

Measuring Municipal Activities C.E. RIDLEY and H.A. SIMON, Chicago: International City Managers' Association, 1938.

Determining Work Loads for Professional Staff in a Public Welfare Agency, with W.R. DIVINE, E.M. COOPER and M. CHERNIN, Berkeley: Bureau of Public Administration, University of California, 1941.

'The Planning Approach in Public Economy', Further Comment, *Quarterly Journal of Economics*, 1941, 55, pp. 325-330.

Fiscal Aspects of Metropolitan Consolidation, Berkeley: Bureau of Public Administration, University of California, 1943.

'New Sources of Municipal Revenues', *Municipal Year Book*, 1943, pp. 254-259.

'The Incidence of a Tax on Urban Real Property', *Quarterly Journal of Economics*, 1943, 57, pp. 398-420.

'Symmetric Tests of the Hypothesis that the Mean of One Normal Population Exceeds that of Another', *Annals of Mathematical Statistics*, 1943, 14, pp. 149-154.

'Decision-making and Administrative Organization', *Public Administration Review*, 1944, 4, pp. 16-32.

'Statistical Tests as a Basis for "Yes–No" Choices', *Journal of the American Statistical Association*, 1945, 40, pp. 80-84.

'What is Urban Redevelopment?', *Illinois Tech Engineer*, December 1946.

Administrative Behavior, New York: Macmillan, 1947.

'Effects of Increased Productivity Upon the Ratio of Urban to Rural Population', *Econometrica*, 1947, 15, pp. 31-42.

'The Axioms of Newtonian Mechanics', *The Philosophical Magazine*, 1947, 38, pp. 888-905.

'Note: Some Conditions of Macroeconomic Stability', D. HAWKINS and H.A. SIMON, *Econometrica*, 1949, 17, pp. 245-248.

'Public Administration', with D.W. SMITHBURG and V.A. THOMPSON, New York: Alfred A. Knopf, 1950.

'The Effects of Atomic Power on National or Regional Economics', in S.H. SCHURR and J. MARSCHAK, eds., *Economic Aspects of Atomic Power*, Princeton: Princeton University Press, 1950.

'Atomic Power and the Industrialization of Backward Areas', in S.H.

SCHURR and J. MARSCHAK, eds., *Economic Aspects of Atomic Power*, Princeton: Princeton University Press, 1950.

'Effects of Technological Change in a Linear Model', in T. KOOPMANS, ed., *Activity Analysis of Production an Allocation*, New York: John Wiley & Sons, 1951.

'The Analysis of Promotional Opportunities', *Personnel*, 1951, 27, pp. 282-285.

'Discussion: The General Theory of Automata', *Econometrica*, 1951, 19, p. 72.

'A Formal Theory of the Employment Relationship', *Econometrica*, 1951, 19, pp. 293-305.

'On the application of Servomechanism Theory in the Study of Production Control', *Econometrica*, 1952, 20, pp. 247-268.

'A Comparison of Organisation Theories', *The Review of Economic Studies*, 1952-1953, 20 (1), pp. 40-48.

'Causal Ordering and Identifiability', in W.C. HOOD and J.C. KOOPMANS, eds., *Studies in Econometric Method*, New York: John Wiley & Sons, 1953.

'Discussion: Decision-making and the Theory of Organization', *Econometrica*, 1953, 21, p. 348.

'Birth of an Organization: The Economic Cooperation Administration', *Public Administration Review*, 1953, 13, pp. 227-236.

'Centralization vs. Decentralization in Organizing the Controller's Department', with G. KOZMETSKY, H. GUETZKOW and G. TYNDALL, New York: The Controllership Foundation, 1954.

'Optimal Decision rules for Production and Inventory Control', C.C. HOLT and H.A. SIMON, *Proceedings of the Conference on Operations Research in Production and Inventory Control*, 1954, pp. 73-89.

'The Control of Inventory and Production Rates', a survey with C.C. HOLT, *Journal of the Operations Research Society of America*, 1954, 2, pp. 289-301.

'Spurious Correlation: A Causal Interpretation', *Journal of the American Statistical Administration*, 1954, 49, pp. 467-479.

'Bandwagon and Underdog Effects and the Possibility of Election Prediction', *Public Opinion Quarterly*, 1954, 18, pp. 245-253.

'Comment: Economic Expectations and Plans of Firms in Relation to

Short-term Forecasting', W.W. COOPER and H.A. SIMON, *Studies in Income and Wealth*, 1955, 17, pp. 352-359.

'A Behavioral Model of Rational Choice', *Quarterly Journal of Economics*, 1955, 69, pp. 99-118.

'Framework of a Theory of the Firm: Comments', in H.R. BOWEN, ed., *The Business Entreprise as a Subject for Research*, ch. 2, Social Science Research Council, Pamphlet, 1955, pp. 43-46.

'Review of "The Mechanism of Economic Systems"', by A. TUSTIN, *Quarterly Review of Applied Mathematics*, 1950, 13, p. 138.

Comportement Organisationel et Comportement rationnel, *Connaissance de l'Homme*, 1955, 13 (12), pp. 87-98.

'Rational Behavior and Organization Theory', in *Trends in Economics*, Conference of Pennsylvania Economists, Pennsylvania State University, 1955, pp. 92-100.

'On a Class of Skew Distribution Functions', *Biometrika*, 1955, 42, pp. 425-440.

'A Linear Decision Rule for Production and Employment Scheduling', C.C. HOLT, F. MODIGLIANI and H.A. SIMON, *Management Science*, 1955, 2, pp. 1-30.

'Dynamic Programming Under Uncertainty with a Quadratic Criterion Function', *Econometrica*, 1956, 24, pp. 74-81.

'Rational Choice and the Structure of the Environment', *Psychological Review*, 1956, 63, pp. 129-138.

'Controlling Inventory and Production in the Face of Uncertain Sales', with C.C. HOLT and F. MODIGLIANI, National Convention Transactions, Montreal, Canada, June 6-8, 1956.

'A Comparision of Game Theory and Learning Theory', *Psychometrika*, 1956, 21, pp. 267-272.

'The Logic Theory Machine', A. NEWELL and H.A. SIMON, *IRE Transactions on Information Theory*, 1956, IT-2 (3), pp. 61-79.

'Observation of a Business Decision', R.M. CYERT, H.A. SIMON and D.B. TROW, *Journal of Business*, 1956, 29, pp. 237-248.

Administrative Behavior, 2nd edn, New York: Macmillan, 1957.

Models of Man, New York: Wiley, 1957.

'The Compensation of Executives', *Sociometry*, 1958, 20, pp. 32-35.

'Empirical Explorations of the Logic Theory Machine: A Case Study in Heuristics', A. NEWELL, J.C. SHAW and H.A. SIMON, in *Proceedings of the Western Joint Computer Conference*, 1957, pp. 218-230.

'Background of Decision Making', *Naval War College Review*, 1957, 10, pp. 1-23.

'Heuristic Problem Solving: The Next Advance in Operations Research', with H.A. SIMON and A. NEWELL, *Operations Research*, 1958, 6, pp. 1-10.

'Selective Perception: A Note on the Department Identification of Executives', D.C. DEARBORN and H.A. SIMON, *Sociometry*, 1958, 21, pp. 140-144.

'The Role of Expectations in an Adaptive or Behavioristic Model', in M.J. BOWMAN, ed., *Expectations, Uncertainty, and Business Behavior*, New York: Social Science Research Council, 1958.

'The Administrator as Decision Maker', *Hospital Administration*, 1958, 3, pp. 26-41.

Il comportamento amministrativo, Italian translation of *Administrative Behavior*, Bologna: Società Editrice Il Mulino, 1958.

The Size Distribution of Business Firms, with C.P. BONINI, *American Economic Review*, 1958, 48, pp. 607-617.

'Chess-playing Programs and the Problem of Complexity', A. NEWELL, J.C. SHAW and H.A. SIMON, *IBM Journal of Research and Development*, 1958, 2, pp. 320-335.

Organizations, J.G. MARCH and H.A. SIMON, New York: Wiley, 1958.

'A Dynamic Model for the Size Distribution of Business Firms', with C.P. BONINI, *Econometrica*, 1958, 26, p. 611.

Theories of Decision-making in Economics and Behavioral Science, *American Economic Review*, 1959, 49, pp. 253-283.

'Some Further Notes on a Class of Skew Distribution Functions', *Information and Control*, 1960, 3, pp. 80-8.

'What Have Computers to Do with Management?' with A. NEWELL, in G.P. SHULTZ and T.L. WHISLER, eds., *Management Organization and the Computer*, Glencoe, IL: The Free Press, 1960.

'Management by Machines: How Much and How Soon?', *The Management Review*, 1960, 49, pp. 12-19, 68-80.

The New Science of Management Decision, New York: Harper & Row, 1960.

Planning Production, Inventories, and Work Force, C.C. HOLT, F. MO-DIGLIANI, J. MUTH and H.A. SIMON, Englewood Cliffs, NJ: Prentice-Hall, 1960.

'The Corporation: Will It be Managed by Machine?', in M. ANSHEN and G.L. BACH, eds., *Management and Corporation*, New York: McGraw-Hill, 1960.

'Simulation of Individual and Group Behavior', G.P.E. CLARKSON and H.A. SIMON, *American Economic Review*, 1960, 50, pp. 920-932.

'Decision Making and Planning', in H.S. PERLOFF, ed., *Planning and the Urban Community*, Pittsburgh: Carnegie Institute of Technnology and the University of Pittsburgh Press, 1961.

'Aggregation of Variables in Dynamic Systems', with A. ANDO, *Econometrica*, 1961, 29, pp. 111-138.

'New Approaches to Decision Processes', part VII, in *Selected Papers From the Workshop in Research Methods, for Directors of University Bureaus of Business and Economic Research*, Urbana: Bureau of Economic and Business Research, University of Illinois, 1961.

'The Decision Maker as Innovator', in S. MAILICK and E.H. VAN NESS, *Concepts and Issues in Administrative Behavior*, Englewood Cliffs, NJ: Prentice-Hall, 1962.

'Strengthening the Behavioral Sciences', *Science*, 1962, 136, pp. 233-241.

'New Developments in the Theory of the Firm', *American Economic Review*, 1962, 52, pp. 1-15.

'The Architecture of Complexity', *Proceedings of the American Philosophical Society*, 1962, 106, pp. 467-482.

'Economics and Psychology', in S. KOCH, ed., *Psychology: A Study of a Science*, vol. 6, New York: McGraw-Hill, 1963.

Some Monte Carlo Estimates of the Yule distribution, with T. VAN WORMER, *Behavioral Science*, 1963, 8, pp. 203-210.

Essays on the Structures of Social Science Models, A. ANDO, F. FISHER and H.A. SIMON, Cambridge, MA: The MIT Press, 1963.

'Discussion: Problems of Methodology', *American Economic Review*, 1963, 53, pp. 229-231.

'A Note on the Cobb–Douglas Function', with F.K. LEVY, *The Review of Economic Studies*, 1963, pp. 93-94.

'Approaching the Theory of Management', in H. KOONTZ, ed., *Toward a Unified Theory of Management*, New York: McGraw-Hill, 1964.

'Comment: Firm Size and Rate of Growth', *Journal of Politcal Economy*, 1964, 72, pp. 81-82.

'A Framework for Decision Making', *Proceedings of a Symposium on Decision Theory*, 1963, 1-9, pp. 22-28.

Business Firm Growth and Size, Y. IJIRI and H.A. SIMON, *American Economic Review*, 1964, 54, pp. 77-89.

'Decision Making as an Economic Resource', in L.H. SELTZER, ed., *New Horizons of Economic Progress. The Franklin Memorial Lectures*, vol. XII, Detroit: Wayne State University Press, 1964.

'Rationality', in J. GOULD and W.L. KOLB, eds., *A Dictionary of the Social Sciences*, Glencoe, IL: The Free Press, 1964.

Appendix: Economics of Milk Production and Distribution in Pennsylvania, H.A. SIMON, J.E. HOLTZINGER, and F.K. MILLER, *Report of the Public Members of the Governor's Milk Control Inquiry Committee, Commonwealth of Pennsylvania*, February 1, 1965.

'Administrative Decision Making', *Public Administration Review*, 1965, 25, pp. 31-37.

The Shape of Automation (For Men and Management), New York: Harper & Row, 1965.

'Political Research: The Decision-Making Framework', in D. EASTON, ed., *Varieties of Political Theory*, Englewood Cliffs, NJ: Prentice-Hall, 1966.

Teoria dell'organizzazione, Italian translation of *Organization*, S. MOSCA, Milano: Edizioni di Comunità, 1966.

'The Automation Bogy', *Dissent*, July-Aug. 1966, pp. 427-429. (Reply to Ben Seligman, and further reply by him.)

'The Impact of New Information Processing Technology', vol. 1, On Managers, vol. 2, On the Economy, *Commercial Letter*, Oct. 1966, Toronto, Imperial Bank of Commerce, pp. 2-12.

'The Business School. A Problem in Organizational Design', *Journal of Management Studies*, 1967, 4, pp. 1-16.

'Programs as Factors of Production', *Proceedings of the 19th Annual Winter Meeting*, 1966, Industrial Relations Research Association, 1967, pp. 178-88.

'Response to an inquiry of research an technical programs, Sub-committee of the Committee on Government Operations, U.S. House of Representative': In 'The Use of Social Research in Federal Domestic programs', part. III, *The Relation of Private Social Scientists to Federal Programs on National Social Problems*, Washington, DC: U.S. Government Printing Office, April 1967, pp. 194ff.

'Information Can be Managed', *Think*, 1967, 33 (3), pp. 8-12.

Il comportamento amministrativo, Italian translation of *Administrative Behavior*, 2nd edn, Bologna: Società Editrice Il Mulino, 1967.

'An Information-Processing Explanation of One-Trial and Incremental Learning', L.W. GREGG and H.A. SIMON, *Journal of Verbal Learning and Verbal Behavior*, 1967, 6, pp. 780-787.

'Testimony: Hearings on a Bill for a National Foundation for the Social Science', Subcommittee on Government Research, Committee on Government Operations, U.S. Senate. Hearing, June 1967, part 2. Washington, DC: U.S. Government Printing Office, 1967, pp. 391-409.

'A model of Business Firm Growth', Y. IJIRI and H.A. SIMON, *Econometrica*, 1967, 35, pp. 348-355.

'Causation', in D.L. SILLS, ed., *International Ecnyclopedia of the Social Sciences* (vol. 2), New York: The Macmillan Company and The Free Press, 1968.

Direzione d'impresa e automazione, Italian translation of *The Shape of Automation*, S. DE VIO and S. PERISSICH, Milano: Etas Kompass, 1968.

'The Future of Information Processing Technology', *Management Science*, 1968, 14, pp. 619-624.

'Research for Choice', in W.R. EWALD, ed., *Environment and Policy: The Next Fifty Years*, Bloomington, IN: Indiana University Press, 1968.

'On Judging the Plausibility of Theories', in B. VAN ROOTSELAAR and J.F. STAAL, eds., *Logic, Methodology and Philosophy of Sciences* III, Amsterdam: North-Holland Publishing Company, 1968.

'Information System for Management in 1942-1967': *Twenty-five Years at RCA Laboratories*, Princeton, NJ: RAC Laboratories, 1968.

The Sciences of the Artificial, Cambridge, MA: The MIT Press, 1969 (Karl Taylor Compton Lectures).

'Man's New Information Environment', *FAR Horizons*, 1969, 2 (3), pp. 1-6.

'Testimony: Hearing on a bill to establish a select senate committee on technology and the human environment', Subcommittee on Intergovernment Relations, U.S. Senate, Washington, DC: U.S. Government Printing Office, 1969, pp. 201-218.

'The Impact of the Computer on Management', Proceeding of the 15th International Management Congress, CIOS, 1969, pp. 25-30.

'Psychology and Economics', with A.C. STEDRY, in G. LINDZEY and E. ARONSON, eds., *The Handbook of Social Psychology*, vol. 5, 2nd edn, Reading, MA: Addison-Wesley, 1979.

'Information Storage as a Problem in Organization Design', in W. GOLDBERG ed., *Behavioral Approaches to Modern Management*, vol. 1, Goteborg: Gothenburg Studies in Businnes Administration, 1970. Reprinted in Ekonomiskt forum, Argang 33, 1970, pp. 46-59.

'Effects of Mergers and Acquisitions on Business Firm Concentration', Y. IJIRI and H.A. SIMON, *Journal of Political Economy*, 1971, 79, pp. 314-322.

'Designing Organizations for an Information-rich World', in M. GREENBERG, ed., *Computers, Communications, and the Public Interest*, Baltimore, MD: The Johns Hopkins Press, 1971.

Human Problem Solving, A. NEWELL and H.A. SIMON, Englewood Cliffs, NJ: Prentice-Hall, 1972.

'Theories of Bounded Rationality', in C.B. MCGUIRE and R. RADNER, ed., *Decision and Organization, A Volume in Honor of Jacob Marschak*, Amsterdam: North-Holland Publishing Company, 1972.

Representation and Meaning: Experiments with Information Processing Systems, with L. SIKLOSSY, ed., Englewood Cliffs, NJ: Prentice-Hall, 1972.

'Central Issues in Designing Management Information Systems', in L. RADANOVIC, ed., *Organization and Computers*, Belgrade: Center for Advanced Studies, 1972.

'Technology and Environment', *Management Science*, 1973, 19, pp. 1110-1121.

'Organizational Man. Rational or Self-actualizing', *Public Administration Review*, 1973, 33, pp. 346-353.

'Rational and/or Self-Actualizing Man' (further reply to Chris Argyris), *Public Administration Review*, 1973, 33, pp. 484-485.

Appendix to 'Residential Choice and Air Pollution: A General Equilibrium Model', E.P. SESKIN and H.A. SIMON, *American Economic Review*, 1973, 63, pp. 966-967.

'Interpretations of Departures From the Pareto Curve Firm-size Distributions', Y. IJIRI and H.A. SIMON, *Journal of Political Economy*, 1974, 82, pp. 315-332.

'Air Quality and Automobile Emission Control', H.A. SIMON, Chairman. A report by the Coordinating Committee on Air Quality Studies, National Academy of Sciences and National Academy of Engineering, vol. 1, Summary Report, U.S. Government Printing Office, September 1974.

'Accounting for Public Services', in Kaikeigaku Hihan (Critical review of accounting theory), edited by an editorial committee. *Essays in Honor of Taminosuke Nishimura*, Tokyo: Chuo Keizai Sha, 1975, pp. 203-209.

'Some Distributions Associated with Bose-Einstein Statistics', Y. IJIRI and H.A. SIMON. *Proceedings of the National Academy of Sciences*, 1975, 72, pp. 1654-1657.

'Optimal Problem-solving Search: All-or-none Solutions', with J.B. KADANE, *Artificial Intelligence*, 1975, 6 (3), pp. 232-247.

Administrative Behavior, 3rd edn, New York: The Free Press, 1976.

'Testimony: Hearing of the House Subcommittee on Sciences, Research and Technology', U.S. House of Representatives. Washington, DC: February 19, 1976.

'Computer Sciences as Empirical Inquiry: Symbol and Search', with A. NEWELL, *Communications of the Association for Computing Machinery*, 1976, 19 pp. 111-126. (1975 ACM Turing Award Lecture).

'The Design of Large Computing Systems as an Organizational Problem', in P. VERBURG, C.A MALOTAUZ, K.T.A. HALBERTSMA and J.L. BOERS, eds., *Organisatiewetenschap en praktijk*. Leiden. H.E. Stenfert Kroese B.V., 1976.

'From Substantive to Procedural Rationality', in S.J. LATSIS, ed., *Method and Appraisal in Economics*, Cambridge: Cambridge University Press, 1976.

The New Science of Management Decision, rev. edn, Englewood Cliffs, NJ: Prentice-Hall, 1977.

Skew Distribution and the Size of Business Firms, with I. IJIRI, Amsterdam: North-Holland Publishing Company, 1977.

'What Computers Mean for Man and Society', *Science*, 1977, 195, pp. 1186-1191.

'Optimal Strategies for a Class of constrained Sequential Problems', J. KADANE and H.A. SIMON, *The Annals of Statistics*, 1977, 5, pp. 237-255.

'The Uses of Mathematics in the Social Sciences', *Proceedings of the First International Conference on Mathematical Modeling*, 1977, 1, pp. 79-90.

Models of Discovery, Boston. D. Reidel Publishing Company, 1977.

Organizing and Managing in an Information-rich Society, English with Japanese translation, Tokyo: Sangyo Nihritusu Tanki Saigaku, 1977.

'Rationality as Process and as Product of Thought', Richard T. ELY lecture, *American Economic Review*, 1978, 68 (2), pp. 1-16.

'Simulation of Large-scale Systems by Aggregation', in R.F. GEYER and J. VAN DER ZOUWEN, eds., *Sociocybernetics*, vol. 2, Leiden: Martinus Nijhoff Social Sciences Division, 1978.

'On how To Decide What To Do', *The Bell Journal of Economics*, 1978, 9, pp. 494-507.

'Are We Alienated From Our Organizations?', *SUPALUM* (School of Urban and Public Affairs Alumni Magazine), 1979, 6 (1), pp. 2-7, Pittsburgh: Carnegie-Mellon University.

Le scienze dell'artificiale, Italian translation of *The Sciences of the Artificial*, P. Unnina, Milano, Istituto Editoriale Internazionale, 1973.

'What is Industrial Democracy?', *Statsvetenskaplig Tidshrift*, 1979, 2, pp. 77-86.

'Rational Decision Making in Business Organization', Nobel Lecture, in *American Economic Review*, 1979, 69, pp. 493-513.

'Fit, Finite and Universal Axiomatization of Theories', *Philosophy of Science*, 1979, 46, pp. 295-301.

Informatica, Direzione Aziendale e Organizzazione del lavoro. Italian translation of *The New Science of Management Decision*, rev. edn, P. MORGANTI, Milano: Franco Angeli Editore, 1979.

'The Consequences of Computers for Centralization and Decentralization', in M.L. DERTOUZOS and J. MOSES, eds., *The Computer Age: A Twenty-year View*, Cambridge, MA: The MIT Press, 1979.

BIBLIOGRAPHY

'Autobiographical Note', in *Les Prix Nobel,* 1978, pp. 271-274. Stockholm: Almqvist and Wiksell International.

Models of Thought, New Haven, CT: Yale University Press, 1979.

'On Parsimonious Explanations of the Production Relation', *The Scandinavian Journal of Economics,* 1979, 81, pp. 459-474.

'Autobiography', in G. LINDZEY, ed., *A History of Psychology in Autobiography* (vol. 7). San Francisco: W.H. Freeman & Company, 1980.

'The Behavioral and Social Sciences', *Science,* 1980, 209, pp. 72-78.

'Behavioral Research: Theory and Public Policy', in *The 1979 Founders Symposium,* The Institute for Social Research: Honoring George Katona, Survey Research Center, Institute for Social Research, The University of Michigan, 1980, pp. 11-36.

'Testimony: hearings before the Subcommittee on Science, Research and Technology of the Committee on Science and Technology', U.S. House of Representatives (National Science Foundation Hearings). Items, 1980, 34 (1), pp. 6-7.

The Sciences of the Artificial (2nd edn), Cambridge, MA: The MIT Press, 1981.

'Prometheus or Pandora: The Influence of Automation on Society', *Computer,* 1981, 14, pp. 69-74.

On the Alienation of Workers and Management, Hamilton, Ontario, McMaster University, 1981. The Zucker Lecture, 1978.

'Unity of the Arts and Sciences: The Psychology of Thought and Discovery', *Bulletin of the American Academy of Arts and Sciences,* 1982, 35, pp. 26-53.

'Are social Problems that Social Science can Solve?', in W. H. KRUSKAL, ed., *The Social Sciences: Their Nature and Uses.* Chicago, IL: The University of Chicago Press, 1982.

Models of Bounded Rationality (2 volumes), Cambridge, MA: The MIT Press, 1982.

'Accurate Predictions and Fixed Point Theorems: Comment (and) Final Comment', *Social Science Information,* 1982, 21: pp. 605-612; 622-626.

Election predictions: Reply, *Inquiry,* 1982, 25, pp. 361-364.

The Rural–Urban Population Balance Again, *Regional Science and Urban Economics,* 1982, 12, pp. 599-606.

'Programs in Public Policy: Issues in Organizational Design' H.A. SIMON and J.P. CRECINE, in J.P. CRECINE, ed., *The new Educational Programs in Public Policy: The First Decade*, Research in public policy analysis and management, Supplement 1. Greenwich, CT: JAI Press, 1982.

The Behavioral Approach: With Emphasis on Economics, R.M. CYERT and H.A. SIMON, *Behavioral Science*, 1983, 28 (2), pp. 95-108.

Reason in Human Affairs, Stanford, CA: Stanford University Press, 1983.

'Fitness Requirements for Scientific Theories', *British Journal for the Philosophy of Science*, 1983, 34, pp. 355-365.

'Mutual Deterrence or Nuclear Suicide', *Science*, 1984, 223 (4638), p. 775.

Protocol Analysis: Verbal Reports as Data, with K.A. ERICSSON, Cambridge, MA: MIT Press, 1984.

'On the Behavioral and Rational Foundations of Economic Dynamics', *Journal of Economic Behavior and Organization*, 1984, 5 (1), pp. 35-55.

La ragione nelle vicende umane, Italian translation of *Reason in human affairs*, Bologna: Il Mulino, 1984. Translated by Giovanni P. del Mistral.

'Cohabiting the Planet with Computers', in J.F. TRAUB, ed., *Cohabiting With Computers*, Los Altos, CA: William Kaufmann, Inc., 1985.

'My Life Philosophy', *The American Economist*, 1985, 29 (1), pp. 15-20.

'Human Nature in Politics: The Dialogue of Psychology with Political science, *American Political Science Review*, 1985, 79, pp. 293-304.

'Maintaining the Peace', in M.D. WARD, ed., *Theories, Models, and Simulations in International Relations*. Essays in Honor of Harold Guetzkow, Boulder, Coloraldo: Westview Press, 1985, pp. 535-548.

'Artificial Intelligence: Current Status and Future Potential', *The Charles H. Davis Lecture Series*, The Naval War College, March 19 and 28, 1985, Washington, DC: The Academy Press, 1985, pp. 24.

'Quantification of Theoretical Terms and the Falsifiability of Theories', *British Journal for the Philosophy of Science*, 1985, 36, pp. 291-298.

Causalità, Razionalità, Organizzazione, Bologna: Il Mulino, 1985, 404 p. Italian translations of 14 published economic papers, translated by Francesco Filippi, Barbara Giorgini and Antonella Minichetti.

'Some Design and Research Methodologies in Business Administration', in M.A. and J.L. MALOUIN, ed., *La production des connaissances scientifiques de l'administration,* Quebec: Les Presses de l'Université Laval, 1986, pp. 239-279.

'Report of the Research Briefing Panel on Decision Making and Problem Solving', *Research Briefings 1986 for the Office of Science and Technology Policy, the National Science Foundation, and selected Federal Departments and Agencies,* Washington: National Academy Press, 1986, pp. 19-35.

'Foreword to "*Corporate Capital Investment: A Behavioral Approach*"' by P. BROMILEY, Cambridge: Cambridge University Press, 1986, pp. 9-10.

'Causality in Device Behavior', Y. IWASAKI and H.A. SIMON, *Artificial Intelligence,* 1986, 29, pp. 3-32.

Reply to Robert W. CLOWER and Mark F. SHAREFKIN. (Reply to their comments on 'On the behavioral and rational foundations of economic dynamics'), in R.H. DAY and G. ELIASSON, eds., *The Dynamics of Market Economies,* Amsterdam: North-Holland, 1986, pp. 48-49.

'The Failure of Armchair Economics' (report of an interview), *Challenge,* November/December 1986, 29 (5), pp. 18-25.

'Rationality in Psychology and Economics', *The Journal of Business,* 1986, 59.

Scientific Discovery: Computational Explorations of the Creative Processes P. LANGLEY, H.A. SIMON, G.L. BRADSHAW and J.M. ZYTKOW. Cambridge, MA: The MIT Press, 1987.

'The Impact of Electronic Communications on Organizations', in R. WOLF, ed., *Organizing Industrial Development,* Berlin: Walter de Gruyter, 1986.

'Charles E. Merriam, and the "Chicago School" of Political Science' *The Edmund James Lecture,* October 10, 1985, Urbana-Champaign, IL: The Department of Political Science University of Illinois, 1987, 11 pp.

Making Management Decisions: The Role of Intuition and Emotion. Academy of Management EXECUTIVE, February 1987, pp. 57-64.

'Così parlò Herbert Simon, Interviewed by Luigi Muscettola', *Industria oggi,* Jan. 1987, 2 (2) pp. 106-111.

'Computers and Society', in S. Kiesler and L. Sproull, eds., *Computing and Change on Campus*, Cambridge, MA: Cambridge University Press, 1987, pp. 4-5.

'The Steam Engine and the Computer: What Makes Technology Revolutionary', *EDUCOM Bullettin*, Spring 1987, 22 (1), pp. 2-5.

'Behavioural Economics', in J. EATWELL, M. MILGATE and P. NEWMAN, eds., *The New Palgrave Dictionary of Economics*, London: Macmillan, 1987, 1, pp. 221-225.

'Bounded Rationality', in J. EATWELL, M. MILGATE, & P. NEWMAN, eds., *The New Palgrave Dictionary of Economics*, London: Macmillan, 1987, 1, pp. 266-268.

'Causality in Economic Models', in J. EATWELL, M. MILGATE and P. NEWMAN, eds., *The New Palgrave Dictionary of Economics*, London: Macmillan, 1987, 1, pp. 382-383.

Evans, Griffith Conrad, in J. EATWELL, M. MILGATE and P. NEWMAN, eds., *The New Palgrave Dictionary of Economics*, London: Macmillan, 1987, 2, pp. 198-199.

'Satisficing', in J. EATWELL, M. MILGATE and P. NEWMAN, eds., *The New Palgrave Dictionary of Economics*, London: Macmillan, 1987, 4, pp. 243-245.

'Politics as Information Processing', *L.S.E. Quarterly*, Winter 1987, 1, pp. 345-370.

'Problem Solving and Reasoning', with J.G. GREEN, in R.C. ATKINSON, R.J. HERRNSTEIN, G. LINDZAY and R.D. LUCE, eds., *Stevens's Handbook of Experimental Psychology*, 2nd edn, vol. II, New York: John Wiley, 1988, pp. 589-672.

Le scienze dell'artificiale, Italian translation of *The Sciences of the Artificial*, (2nd edn), Bologna: Il Mulino, 1988. Translated by Anna Trani, Introduction by Paolo Legrenzi.

'Causal Ordering, Comparative Statics, and Near Decomposability', with Y. Iwasaki, *Journal of Econometrics*, 1988, 39, pp. 149-173.

'The jxperts in Your Midst', with M. Prietula, *Harvard Business Review*, Jan.-Feb., 1989, pp. 120-124.

'Managing in an Information Rich World', in Y.K. SHETTY and V.M. BUEHLER, eds., *Competing Through Productivity and Quality*, Cambridge, MA: Productivity Press, 1988, pp. 45-54.

'The Scientist as Problem Solver' in D. KLAHR and K. KOTOVSKY, eds., *Complex Information Processing*: Essays in honor of Herbert A. Simon., Hillsdale, NJ: Lawrence Erlbaum Associates, 1989.

Models of Thought: vol. II, New Haven. CT: Yale University Press, 1989.

'Why Economist Disagree', *Journal of Business Administration*, 1988/89, 18 (1 and 2), pp. 1-19.

'The State of Economic Science', in W. SICHEL, ed., *The State of Economic Science*: Views of Six Nobel Laureates, Kalamazoo, MI: W.E. Upjohn Institute for Employment Research, 1989.

'Prediction and Prescription in Systems Modeling', *Operations Research*, 1990, 38, pp. 7-14.

'Bounded Rationality and the Theory of the Firm': An Interview with Herbert A. Simon, *Annali scientifici del dipartimento di economia dell'Università degli Studi di Trento*, 1989, pp. 41-70.

'Testimony, National Science and Technology Policy, U.S. Senate Committee on Commerce, Science and Transportation', Subcommittee on Science, Technology and Space. Senate Hearing 7 1989, pp. 249-269.

'Large Organizations in Modern Society', *Il Politico: Rivista Italiana di Scienze Politiche*, 1989, 54, pp. 545-551.

'Laboratory Replication of Scientific Discovery Processes', with Y. QIN, *Cognitive Science*, 1990, 14, pp. 281-312.

'Remarks in: Seminario su "Il contributo di Herbert A. Simon alle scienze sociali contemporanee"', *Il Politico: Rivista Italiana di Scienze Politiche*, 1989, 54, pp. 671-673.

'Human Experts and Knowledge-based System', in M. TOKORO, Y. ANZAI and A. YONEZAWA, eds., *Concepts and Characteristc of Knowledge-based Systems*, Amsterdam: North-Holland, 1989.

Interview: 'Tra razionalità e cognizione', *Rassegna Italiana di Sociologia*, 1990, 31 (1), pp. 3-10

'A Mechanism for Social Selection and Successful Altruism', *Science*, 1990, 250, pp. 1665-1668.

Models of My Life, New York: Basic Books, 1991.

'Bounded Rationality and Organizational Learning', *Organizational Science*, 1991, 2, pp. 125-134.

'The Mathematical Bases for Qualitative Reasoning', with J. KALAGNANAM and Y. YWASAKI, *IEEE Expert*, 1991, 6, pp. 11-19.

'Organizations and Markets', *Journal of Economic Perspectives*, 1991, 5, pp. 25-44.

'Problems Representation', in R.F. RASHID, ed., *CMU Computer Science*, A 25th Anniversary Commemorative, New York: ACM Press, 1991, pp. 449-463.

Public Administration, New Brunswick, NJ: Transaction Publishers, 1991. Reprint of 1950 edition, with new introduction, pp. xiii-xxi.

'Problem Formulation and Alternative Generation in the Decision Making Process', in A. CHIKAN, *et al.*, eds., *Progress in Decision, Utility and Risk Theory*, Boston, MA: Kluwer, 1991, pp. 77-84.

'Effect of Mode of Data Presentation on Reasoning About Economic markets', in H. TABACHNECK, *American Association for Artificial Intelligence Spring Symposium Series*: Working Notes, 1992,

Economics, Bounded Rationality, and the Cognitive Revolution, with M. EGIDI, R. MARRIS and R. VIALE, edited by M. Egidi and R. Marris. Brooksfield, VT: Edward Elgar, 1992. (A colloquium, four reprinted papers, commentaries by Egidi, Marris and Viale).

Interview with Carla Ravioli (excerpts), in C. RAVIOLI, *Il pianeta degli economisti ovvero l'economia contro il pianeta* (in italian), Torino, Italy: Isedi, 1992.

'Methodological Foundations of Economics', in J.L. AUSPITZ, W.W. GASPARSKI, M.K. MLICKI and K. SZANIAWSKI, eds., *Praxiologies and the Philosophy of Economics*, New Brunswick, NJ: Transaction Publishers, 1992.

'Altruism and Economics', *Eastern Economic Journal*, 18 (1), 1992, pp. 73-83.

'What is an "Explanation" of Behavior?', *Psychological Science*, 1992, 3, pp. 150-161.

Protocol Analysis: Verbal Reports as Data (rev. edn) with K.A. ERICSSON, Cambridge, MA: The MIT Press, 1993.

'Altruism and Economics', *The American Economic Review, Papers and Proceedings of the 105th Annual Meeting of the American Economic Association*, 1993, 83 (2), pp.156-161.

'Organizations', 2nd edn, with J.G. MARCH, Cambridge, MA: David Blackwell, 1993.

BIBLIOGRAPHY

'Decision Making: Rational, Nonrational, and Irrational', *Educational Administration Quarterliy*, 1993, 29, pp. 392-411.

'Satisficing', in D. GREENWALD, ed., *The McGraw-Hill Encyclopedia of Economics*, 2nd edn, New York: McGraw-Hill, Inc., 1993.

'The Human Mind: The Symbolic Level', *Proceedings of the American Philosophical Society*, 1993, 137, pp. 638-647.

'Adaptive Strategies in Thought Processes', *Comunicazioni Scientifiche di Psicologia Generale, Nuova serie*, Università degli Studi di Roma 'La Sapienza', Facoltà di Psicologia, Edizioni Scientifiche Italiane, 127 p., 1993.

'Is International Management Different from Management?', *Working Paper no. 94-1, Carnegie Bosch Institute for Applied Studies in International Management*, Carnegie Mellon University, Graduate School of Industrial Administration. Talk given at Stuttgart, May 14, 1993.

'Fitness Requirements for Scientific Theories Containing Recursive Theoretical Terms', with W. SHEN, *British Journal for the Philosophy of Science*, 1993, 44, pp. 641-652.

'Strategy and Organizational Evolution', *Strategic Management Journal*, 1993, 14, pp. 131-142.

'Causality and Model Abstraction', with Y. IWASAKI, *Artificial Intelligence*, 1994, 67, pp. 143-194.

'Bottleneck of Attention: Connecting Thought with Motivation', in W.D. SPAULDING, ed., *Integrative Views of Motivation, Cognition, and Emotion*, Lincoln, NE: University of Nebraska Press, 1994.

INDEX

INDEX

Abstraction 11, 61-2
agents
  intentional actions 146
  preferences 147-8
aggregation problems 72-3, 174
Alchian 104
alienation 59
Allais 147-8, 171
Allen 104
altruism 33
  in economics 42-3
  hostility and 54-5
  neo-Darwinian theory and 39-42,
    176-7
  organizational identification as 38-45,
    48, 52
  rationality and 57-8
  utility 10
Anderson, J. R. 81, 121, 161 n. 183
Ando, A. 194
Angell, N. 192
animal spirits 15-16, 36
Arcangeli, F. 94
Arrow, A. K. 3, 17, 117, 193
artificial intelligence 68-9, 122, 163
assumptions
  neoclassical theory 14-15, 21
  satisficing versus optimizing 69-70,
    107
  strong versus weak 69-70
  tested 21, 23, 155

Bacdayan, P. 121
Bach, G. L. 194
BACON 99
Barone, E. 113, 115
Baylor 185
Becker, G. S. 31, 69
belief reliability 159 n.
biology 30
Black, J. 99
Block, N. 159 n.
bounded rationality 3
  and artificial intelligence 68-9
  compared to global rationality 17-18,
    25, 154-5
  docility and 41

empirical evidence 22, 90
Hayek to Simon 116-19
influence on behavior 45, 186
macroeconomics and 133, 138
in managerial economics 107
normative aspect of 156-60
objective concept 26-7
origin of idea 16
Smith's 20
unemployment and 70
unpredictability and 66
Bouwman, M. J. 81
Bradshaw 98
Bromiley, p. 82-3
Brown, H. G. 21

Capital 7
Chamberlin, E. 75
Chandler, A. 84
Charnes, A. 82
Cherniak, C. 159 n.
choice theory 13-17
choice under uncertainty 78-9
Clarkson, G. P. E. 81
Coase 104, 111-12, 115, 118, 141, 176
Coase Theorem 21
Cohen, M. D. 121
Colby, K. 182
common sense 20-1, 22, 31, 63
Commons, J. R. 191
competition 117, 127
competitive selection 132
computer programs 80-1, 185-6
connectionist theories 181-2
contracts
  employment 46, 47
  enforceability 34-5, 48
  goods and services 47
  information neede 47-8
Cooper, W. W. 82, 194
cooperation 105, 126, 127
coordination 48-9, 52, 111-15, 116-19,
    176-8
Copernicus 5
Cournot, A. A. 9
creative destruction 125-6
Cyret, R. M. 82, 119, 194

Darwinian fitness 39-41
data
    implications for theory 63-70
    noise 72
    organizational identification 64
    sources 70-1, 84-8
    statistical 72
    verbal protocol 79-81
    see also empirical 72
Dearborn, D.C. 64, 95
Debreu, G. 147-8, 171
decision making
    case studies 81-4
    centralized and decentralized 50, 52,
        114-15
    collective 108-9
    deliberation in 10
    methods 71
    in organizations 119
    rationality 156-7
demand curves 69
Dematté, C. 103-9, 169, 176-8
design tasks 51, 106, 123-4
Devitt, M. 159 n.
discovery of alternatives 98-9
division of labor 46, 104, 127, 176
docility 41-2, 58, 108
Doll 136

Econometrics 23, 72-4, 95-7
economic structure 134, 143
economics
    applied 86, 89
    contradicts facts 136
    data implications 63-70
    defined 13
    experimental 74-8, 137
    and great books 134
    guide to action 62-3
    new institutional 13, 33, 39, 104, 108,
        128
    normative 67-9
    revolutionary 86-7
    see also macroeconomics
Edgeworth, F. Y. 21
efficiency 13, 49-51
Egidi, M. 111-33, 141, 159 n., 169, 177-8
Einstein, A. 182
Ellsberg 148, 171
Ely 192
empirical evidence 22, 90, 155

Smith's 19-20, 28
    see also data; experimental economics;
        laboratory studies
empirical tests 22-3
employment contract 46, 47
employment relation 34-5
enterpreneur 36
EPAM 178, 183-4, 183-4
equilibrium
    evolutive and reflective 157-8 n.
    general 116
Ericsson, K. A. 80
executive compesation 67
expectations 10, 15-16, 36
experimental economics 74-8, 137
    see also data; empirical evidence;
        laboratory studies
expert systems 68

Feyerabend, P. K. 4
Field, H. 159 n.
firms, theory of 176-8
    boundaries 38, 48, 115
    case studies 81-4
    growth rates 65-6, 142-4
    nature of 36, 103
    size 65-6, 139-42, 175-6
    see also organizations
forecasting models 16
Freud, S. 26
Friedman, M. 25, 29, 61-2, 155, 173, 193
Frisch, 193

Galileo 4-5, 29, 61
game theory 75-6
George, H. 192
Gibrat 142-4
global rationality
    compared to bounded rationality
        17-18, 25, 154-5
    Marshall's 20-1
    not achievable 40
    and unemployment 22
Goodman, N. 157 n.
Goodwin, R. 169, 174
Grandori, A. 54, 94
Guetskow, H. 94
    guilt 42

Haavelmo 73
Hart, A. G. 16

Hart, P. 142
Hawkins, D. 194
Hayek, von F. A. 37, 48, 50, 112, 114, 116-19
Hicks, J. 193
Hinton, G. 163 n.
Hirschman, A. O. 128
history
    data source 84-5
    whiggish 3-4, 175
Hogarth, R. 161 n.
Holland, J. M. 159 n.
Holt, C. C. 82, 194
Holyoak, K. J. 159 n.
homo oeconomicus 153-4
honesty 12
Hood, W. C. 73
hostile mergers 136-7
hostility 54-5
Hurwicz, L. 193
Hutchinson 154-5

Ichino, A. 25, 54, 94
identification problem 73, 96-7
Ijiri, Y. 65-6, 142, 195
inference rules 94-5
information 47-8, 52, 114-15, 177-8
institutions, artificial and natural 118
instrumentalism 155, 173

Jensen 142
Jevons, H. S. 9
joint stock companies 6, 12

Kahneman, D. 78. 171
Katona, G. 88
Kepler 99
Keynes, J. M. 14-15, 22, 36, 56, 70, 133-4,
    138, 169, 175, 193
Keynes, N. 154
Klein, L. 193
Knight, F. H. 14, 16, 104
knowledge 115, 127
    division of 122-7
    role of 116
Koopmans, T. C. 73, 193
Kosslyn, S. 182
Kripke, S. 159 n.
Kuhn, T. S. 86-7

Laboratory studies
    of markets 74-8

problem solving 79-81
    see also data; empirical evidence;
        experimental economics
Laird, J. 163
Lakatos 155
Lange, O. 193
Langley 98
Lasswell, H. 192
Laudan, L. 165
learning 112, 116-19
    organizational 119-27
linear programming 67-8
logical coherence 158-9 n.
Lucas 22, 70, 133
Lycan, W. 159 n.

McClellan, J. 184
McGinn, C. 159 n.
macroeconomics
    and bounded rationality 133, 138
    and microeconomics 12-14, 133-8
March, J. G. 82, 118-20, 127, 194
marginal concepts 9
markets
    laboratory studies of 74-8
    and Pareto efficiency 70
    role 38
    versus firms 33-8, 46-9, 103, 111-15
Marris, R. 54, 133-44, 159 n., 169, 174-6,
    178
Marschak, J. 193
Marshall, A. 9-14, 20, 27, 70-1, 134,
    139-40, 169, 175
Mater 185-6
Meade, J. 193
Meckling 142
mental process
    models 179-80
    slow 179
Merkel, H. 191-2
Merriam, C. 192
meta rules 122
Michelson-Morley experiment 79
Mill, J. S. 153-4, 156
Mises, von L. 114, 155
Modigliani, F. 82, 193-4
money 11, 15
Montesano, A. 145-53, 169-74
Morgenstern, O. 75
motivation 182
    component of loyalty 44-5

of managers 141
wealth seeking 38-9, 51-2
within organizations 57-8
Muth, J. F. 82, 194

Nelson, R. R. 36, 120
neoclassical theory 56
assumptions 14-15, 21
described 145
inadequacies 89-90, 150
non-trivial results 149
and rationality 25, 145-8
and reality 29
too demanding 172
uses of 170
neural networks 164, 180
Neumann, von J. 9
Newell, A. 119, 183, 194
Newton, I. 30, 184
Neyman, J. 193
Nisbett, R. E. 88, 158-9 n.
non-linear equations 174
North, D. C. 86

Opportunism 127-31
organization ownership 52
relative efficiency 49-51
organization-centric view 35-6
organizational design 51, 106, 123-4
organizational identification 95
and altruism 38-45, 48, 52, 108
data 64
and loyalty 43-5
organizational loyalty 33, 59, 105
identification 43-5
limits to 129-31
and opportunism 127-31
organizations
interaction with markets 37-8
reasons for existence 46-9, 104-7
role of 6
versus markets 33-8, 46-9, 103, 111-15
see also firms

Pareto, V. 134
Pasinetti, L. 25
Patinkin, D. 193
perceptive rationality 156, 158
physics 29-30
Pierson 21
Planck 79

planning 123-4, 178
central 51, 114, 118
Polanyi, M. 120
policy issues 10, 56
Prais, S. 142
price system 37
priors 73-4, 77
problem solving 79-81
procedural rationality 3, 8, 18-19, 22, 26
procedures 120-2
production systems 161-2, 181, 184-5
production technology 106
profit motive 51-2
psychology 161-4
advances in 137-8, 178-87
cognitive revolution 79
experimental 76-7
use of 98
public goods problem 59
Putnam, H. 159 n.
Pye, D. 195

Qualitative evidence 97
Quine 165

R-squares 96
Rashevsky, N. 192
rationality
and altruism 57-8
the concept 3-13, 26-7, 165-6
definition 75
hidden forms 57-8
in Marshall's Principles 9-13
and neoclassical theory 145-8
perceptive 156, 158
plurality of 17-19, 25-6
postulate tests 78-9
procedural 3, 8, 18-19, 22, 26
and selfishness 10
substantive 3, 18
in The Wealth of Nations 5-9
see also bounded rationality
reasoning reliability 171
Reder, M. 161 n.
Rees, A. 13-14
Ridley, C. E. 192
risk aversion 106
rivalry 126
Robbins, L. C. 155
Roberts, D. R. 67
Ross, L. 159 n.
routine behavior 120-2
Russia 45

Samuelson, P. A. 193
savings 8
Schultz, H. 192-3
Schumpeter, J. A. 36, 119, 125-6
science
    experimental and theoretical 85, 87
    history 4-5, 135
    revolutionary 87
    verification 135-6
self-interest 6, 7-8, 10, 19, 27
Seligman 21
Senior, N. W. 154
sensitivity 21
shame 42
shirking 44, 128
Simon, H. A. 34-5, 40, 45, 65-6, 80, 98,
    118-20, 147
Singley, M. K. 121
Smith, A. 3, 5-10, 12-13, 19, 22, 27, 37, 46,
    70-1, 84, 105, 111, 134, 153, 174
Smith, V. 23, 75
Squire, L. R. 121
Sterelny, K. 159 n.
Stich, S. 158 n., 160 n.
stylized facts 95, 96
subconscious and unconscious 178-9, 182
substantive rationality 3, 18
survey techniques 88-9
symbolic systems 182-3, 185

Terlizzese, D. 54, 94
Thagards, P. R. 159 n.
theory
    of the mind 26
    parsimony 70, 108
    role of 55-6

Theil 194
Thuenen, von J. H. 9
Tiebout, C. M. 21
Tinbergen 94
tit-for-tat strategy 76
Trow, D. B. 119
Turing, A. 162, 184-5
Tversky, A. 78, 171

Uncertainty 16
unemployment 22, 70, 175
universities 49-50
unpredictability 66
utility
    in altruism 10
    function 8, 13, 137-8
    maximization 11, 13, 31, 170-1, 172
    theory 42-3

Viale, R. 133, 153-66, 169, 173, 178,
    180-6
virtuous and adverse selection 131-2

Wages 6-7
Walras, L. 112, 115
Walrasian model 112-15
whiggish history 3-4, 27
Whigs 134-5
Wien 79
Williamson, O. 35, 38, 47, 125-6, 176
Wilson, T. D. 88
Winter, S. 36, 120
Wold, H. 94

Zappa, G. 104
Zykow 98